MODERN MEDITATIONS

NICHIKO NIWANO

M·O·D·E·R·N
MEDITATIONS
A BUDDHIST SAMPLER

translated by
Richard L. Gage
and
Jeffrey Hunter

KOSEI PUBLISHING CO. · TOKYO

Editorial supervision by EDS Inc., Editorial &
Design Services. Book design, typography, and cover
design by Becky Davis, EDS Inc. The text of this book
is set in a computer version of Palatino with a
computer version of Palatino for display.

Cover photograph by David Beatty
and Susan Griggs/PPS.

First edition, 1990
Second printing, 1991

Published by Kōsei Publishing Co.,
Kōsei Building, 2-7-1 Wada, Suginami-ku, Tokyo 166, Japan.
Copyright © 1990 by Kōsei Publishing Co.; all
rights reserved. Printed in Japan.

ISBN 4-333-01477-8
LCC Card No. applied for

CONTENTS

Prologue   7

BRINGING RELIGION TO LIFE   11

Practicing Faith   13
Discovering the Meaning of Practice   22
Finding Spiritual Satisfaction   29
Practicing Charity   36
Acquiring Virtue   43
Being Truly Happy   50

MAKING THE MOST OF OURSELVES   57

Taking Up Challenges   59
Remedying Shortcomings   66
Gaining Through Adversity   71
Knowing Ourselves   77
Developing Mental Flexibility   85
Learning to Be Teachers   92

BUILDING HARMONY 99

Bringing Out the Best in Others   101
Understanding Others   107
Being Considerate   114
Guiding the Young   120
Raising Children   127
Balancing Work and Rest   135
Living with Nature   142

PROLOGUE

When we try to imagine what our world will be like in the future, we tend to have grand dreams and hopes. We wonder how society will change, what daily life will be like. Yet as we see from the fast pace of life today, society is already undergoing a dizzying transformation.

We will be greeting the twenty-first century in just a few years. We know that the dawn of a new century does not mean that the world will greatly change, but still we cannot help hoping the future will be brighter.

When we look around us today, however, we see a world plagued by destruction of the natural environment, acid rain, an increase in atmospheric carbon dioxide and other gases creating the greenhouse effect, a worsening population explosion, the depletion of our fossil fuel resources, and the arms race. The bright future that we envision is dimmed by these perilous conditions that spell danger not only for the human race but also for our planet itself, and we are forced to contemplate a bleaker future.

Scientific progress has improved our quality of life, making it more pleasant and convenient. Yet our incessant desires drive us in pursuit of even greater pleasure and convenience, and we are now about to permanently damage the global environment, on which our very survival depends.

Many countries are adopting measures to protect the environment, such as developing technologies to prevent pollution and undertaking projects to arrest desertification. But destruction of the environment is proceeding faster than we imagine, and the problems besetting our environment are more serious than we think.

When we trace environmental problems to their source, we always come to the way in which people live. In that it teaches us to live in a way that allows us to solve these problems, religion will play a vital role in the future.

There is good and bad in everything, and as civilization's benefits are great, so are its evils, such as the destruction of our environment. With the growth of our material prosperity, these problems will become more severe, and no comprehensive solution is in sight.

To live in harmony with nature, it is important that we accept the universal truths that are acknowledged by all religions and follow the teaching of the historical Buddha, Shakyamuni, that we should be satisfied with little. When every member of the human race recognizes this, the global environment will be preserved in true harmony and a peaceful world supported by trust will be built. That is why the twenty-first century is expected to be a century of religion, in which the task of consoling and comforting those who suffer will fall to religious believers.

The universal truths that Buddhism teaches as guides for living can be summed up in the two statements "All things are impermanent" and "All things are interrelated." The tenets of Buddhism can also be epitomized as teachings on life and death—the unalterable reality that everything that lives must die. In his great compassion, the Buddha teaches us to live our lives in a meaningful way, so that we regret nothing.

The way we go about living differs according to whether we truly consider the meaning of life and death or ignore it; thus our lives naturally differ, too. If we think deeply about life and death, we realize that our own existence is the product of an immeasurable chain of ancestors and that we live each day dependent on both a vast number of other people and our global environment. Though we may think we live by our own efforts alone, life is in fact a gift. As we deepen our awareness of this, we recognize the dignity of life and the marvel that all living beings coexist with one another's help.

When we view life in this spirit, we realize that true happiness and peace of mind are achieved through not desiring too much, through being satisfied with what we have, through not thinking only of ourselves, and through serving others (what Mahayana Buddhism terms "the bodhisattva practice"), so that eventually we wish to serve others and undertake bodhisattva practice of our own accord. For Buddhists this realization entails not only cultivating and practicing a way of seeing and thinking that allows us to live as human beings should but also sharing this realization with those who have not yet had the opportunity to encounter the teachings of the Buddha, so that they too may find happiness.

The people of the world are now seeking religion. Religious believers must hear their urgent cries and respond, working as hard as possible. Such efforts also contribute to the discovery of our own purpose in life.

It will take a long time to restore the global environment, learn to live once again in harmony with nature, and build trust among all human beings. Yet if we only look on and wring our hands, nothing will improve in the least; we will simply move further along the road to destruction.

When people are driven by necessity, they finally awaken to reality and seek truth. It is important that those who awaken act. With faith and commitment, they must awaken the same faith and commitment in others in every part of the world. For Buddhists, this means that all of us, as individuals, must pray for peace as we devote ourselves to spreading our faith, fostering interreligious cooperation, and fulfilling our daily responsibilities. We must go forth to light the lamp of the Buddha's teachings in the heart of one person after another.

BRINGING RELIGION TO LIFE

PRACTICING FAITH

During a visit to Japan some years ago, Mother Teresa of Calcutta commented that while probably no one dies of hunger in materially blessed Japan, Tokyo impressed her as being spiritually impoverished in many respects. It does seem that, obsessed by immediate profit, desire, and the needs of the ego, many people today lose sight of the finest and most beautiful things in life. Real happiness is impossible without spiritual fulfillment.

Deep down, even the most egoistic person is endowed with human warmth and longs for true spiritual contact with others. The more spiritually impoverished the times, the more important is what Mother Teresa calls the practice of love—in Mahayana Buddhist terms, the bodhisattva practice of compassionate caring.

Most people are considerate of their family and loved ones, yet seem unable to extend the same concern to people they dislike or find incompatible. But as is taught in chapter 25 of the Lotus Sutra,

"The All-Sidedness of the Bodhisattva Regarder of the Cries of the World," people with the true spirit of universal compassion must be willing to teach and guide all others. Associating with others solely on the basis of personal likes and dislikes can earn one a reputation for exclusivity. That is why all of us should examine our motives to determine whether we are considerate only of people we like.

Good or bad, we are all the Buddha's children. Unless we keep this in mind, we will tend to judge others by our own criteria; such judgments are the most frequent cause of favoritism. From the Buddha's standpoint, each person is born to fill some necessary role. There is bound to be something good even in someone whose faults are obvious and who is therefore frowned upon by the people around him or her. Religious people must believe in that good and, striving to improve their own attitudes, must try hard to discern it.

Caring is essentially a parental attribute. As the Lotus Sutra teaches, the Buddha regards all people as his children and longs to help them improve themselves as much as possible. Never seeking anything in return even for his utmost exertions, the Buddha wishes for every child's happiness and finds fulfillment in seeing each child develop.

Though there are good and bad points in every personality, parents should love all their children equally. Mischievous children are scolded in the hope they will grow into better people and be popular with others. The good things children do are their parents' joy and delight. When their child is ill, many parents forget their own ailments to take care of the child, with whom they would most gladly change places if they could. All this is simply because parents are caring, concerned for their beloved children.

When this kind of parental concern goes beyond the family, it becomes the practice of caring. Warm acts of kindness arising from such concern are especially needed in our egoistic era of spiritual hunger. But it is important to remember that people can sense immediately when kindness is not genuine. Few people, in spite of their spiritual hunger, welcome feigned kindness. They turn away from feigned kindness, which is only for effect. Consequently, it is important to be genuinely concerned and to put ourselves in the other person's place while doing our best to be considerate and helpful.

In the final analysis, everything that Buddhists do should be part of the practice of caring, since acts of any other kind are not in keeping with what is best in human nature. Furthermore, even though those who do good may be convinced they are doing their best, it is unworthy of true Buddhists to perform acts of kindness only because of what others might say or to discriminate among people they have arbitrarily decided are good or bad.

Each time we hear or see the words "the practice of caring," we must examine our own thoughts and actions and try to determine whether they are in keeping with what a person of faith, a person privileged to know the Buddha's teachings, ought to think and do. The caring and kindness that we demonstrate should be the gauge of our progress in the practice of faith. And when we have become even slightly better human beings, faith will bring us true happiness.

❦   ❦   ❦

To make the Buddha's teachings part of our innermost being and to live in a Buddhist way, true to the best of our capabilities, we must daily, consistently study the mind of the Buddha and put what we learn into practice. Repeating the cycle over and over, deepening faith through practice, is the way to approach the supreme goal of buddhahood in this life.

Action and spirit are inseparable in Buddhist practice, but I will examine them separately here. Though many of my fellow Buddhists may still be uncertain of the exact meaning of Buddhism, they enthusiastically read and recite the scriptures each day and train themselves in faith according to guidance and instruction provided by people of greater experience.

Since they do not fully understand Buddhism, they practice it only in their acts. Such practice is nonetheless very important. Obviously it is best to practice faith with full comprehension of the true meaning of our actions. But waiting to achieve this degree of understanding before putting faith into practice could mean a lifetime spent doing nothing. Nowadays especially, many people understand

Buddhism but fail to put that understanding into practice.

First practice faith and, through acting, you will come to comprehend its value and blessedness. Do not look down on the practice of faith expressed in action alone: practically everyone who has an advanced understanding of Buddhism began with just such practice.

Very often the meaning of acts performed by rote becomes apparent much later. For example, someone might read and recite the scriptures faithfully every day without full comprehension but gradually memorize them. As time passes and the person gains more experience in life, that person may suddenly one day grasp their full meaning. A noted writer has said that it was not until he had grown old that he fully savored the meaning of a passage he had learned in youth: "It is easy to grow old but hard to grow wise; make the best of every moment."

When—through practicing faith by doing good deeds—people come to understand the mind of the Buddha and to see things the way the Buddha does, they begin to exert a good influence on everyone they encounter. The Buddhist way of seeing things is a realization both of the buddha-nature, or potential for enlightenment, inherent in all people and of the knowledge that the Buddha employs all kinds of phenomena to instruct us in the way to attain supreme enlightenment.

Those who adopt this way of thinking are able

to discover limitless possibilities in people from the most diverse backgrounds and can influence them to make full use of their potential. These efforts reflect the true spirit of the practice of faith.

Practicing Buddhism means meeting others and acquainting them with the Buddha's way of seeing and interpreting. People who adopt that way of thinking manifest the mind of the Buddha. This is not an easy state to achieve.

As long as we think in ordinary ways, we tend to judge others on the basis of prejudice, emotion, or self-interest. Although clear-cut judgments of right and wrong are essential in building a wholesome society, passing judgment on other people is not the Buddha's way and cannot help us bring them to true salvation.

Religious faith is not a matter of passing judgment on evil. Evildoers know better than anyone else that they are doing wrong. By heeding the conscience that each of us possesses, such people can control their wrongdoing. The role of religious faith is to awaken people to this conscience. As many people have learned, once awakened to the conscience, a person thought incorrigible may show fine traits of character.

We must all strive to be the kind of people who manifest the true spirit of practicing faith. Instead of making judgments on the basis of appearances, people who manifest this spirit see the good in others. Instead of criticizing others' shortcomings, they recognize and try to encourage others' efforts at self-improvement. Even the lives of paupers who view the world in this way are rich with purpose. A life of such richness is open to anyone who strives and who assiduously puts faith into practice.

❦   ❦   ❦

Everyone has a function in society. By working hard to fulfill our roles at home and on the job, we find joy and purpose in being alive. By realizing this and sincerely doing our best every day, we can discover what human life is all about.

But great things cannot be achieved overnight; they take time. Starting out slowly and moving ahead steadily and surely leads first to self-confidence and finally to true ability and power. This is why people usually become good at things they enjoy doing. Though clumsy when beginning something new, they stick to it because it gives them pleasure. As time passes they acquire skill, which intensifies their enjoyment.

Repeating the same task over and over can be tedious and demands perseverance. Failure to progress as desired or to produce satisfying results often makes us want to give up. But overcoming that temptation and sticking to the job can result in unexpected discoveries and joy. As is often said, perseverance is power. For example, herbal medicine is effective only when employed methodically over a long period. In practicing faith, too, we can approach our ideal only by persevering wholeheartedly.

The tendency of modern, science-oriented civilization to demand immediate results diminishes our ability to persevere and tolerate hardship. This is especially true of young people obsessed with the present moment, who overlook fundamental aspects of life.

Broadly speaking, the hedonistic, materialistic pursuit of pleasure and convenience upsets the magnificent harmony of nature and results in environmental pollution. Here, as in all other matters, the long view is of the essence. For instance, it would be foolish to ruin one's stomach with overdoses of over-the-counter drugs. Technological and spiritual growth require foresight, steady effort, and respect for nature and truth.

Practically everything we do requires steady effort. It is said that in terms of ability we are divided into three categories: those who succeed without trying, those who can move steadily ahead if they try, and those who succeed only through bitter struggle. Most of us belong in the second or third category. Not even Confucius, one of the great sages of the world, falls into the first category.

Each of us is good at some things and poor at others. Obviously, nothing is more fortunate than finding an occupation perfectly suited to one's talents. But things do not always turn out this way. Nonetheless, the person who perseveres patiently can discover interest, pleasure, and even joy in work that at first seemed distasteful. Repeated practice and daily effort are the key to attaining this frame of mind.

It is characteristic of human beings to want to be

creative, to progress, and to improve. We make many mistakes along the upward path. But if we adopt the positive approach of learning from our mistakes, they bring opportunities for further self-improvement. Progress requires always keeping goals in view and putting faith into practice without fear of making mistakes.

DISCOVERING THE MEANING
OF PRACTICE

In Buddhist terminology, the realm of nirvana is called "the opposite shore." The opposite shore is enlightenment, a state of mind in which one is free and autonomous and has transcended all suffering and delusion. It is, in other words, the realm of the Buddha. In contrast, the world of delusion in which we live—the world of ignorant, ordinary human beings who are confused and shaken by the changes in their lives—is called "this shore."

The great purpose of Buddhism is to ferry all people from this shore, the world of delusion, to the opposite shore, the realm of nirvana. We tend to think of the two shores as absolutely separate, divided as if by a river. But both are part of earthly existence and thus are joined. Likewise, delusion and enlightenment are indivisible. They are like nested concave and convex forms. If we look at delusion from another angle, it is a manifestation of the desire for salvation and enlightenment.

The greater our delusion, the stronger our desire

for enlightenment and salvation. The worse our delusion, the more depressed we are. But without delusion, the wish for salvation and enlightenment would not arise. People are deluded precisely because they have the ability to solve all sorts of problems; and for the same reason, they have the power to rid themselves of delusion.

We can see that delusion and enlightenment, just like this shore and the opposite shore, make up a whole. When we awaken to this, we also realize that we are all essentially saved already. For Buddhists, it is daily religious practice that carries us from one shore to the other. But rather than say that our practice ferries us across, it is perhaps more accurate to say that it awakens us naturally to our true selves.

For those with faith in the Lotus Sutra, chanting the name of the sutra is a declaration of their commitment to absolute truth. It is a commitment quite unrelated to intellectual accomplishments. It expresses an awakening to our true selves and to the reality of our already having been saved. In our daily practice we move step by step through repeated cycles of delusion and enlightenment toward fulfillment of the Buddha's original vow that everyone will attain buddhahood.

Unfortunately, once people begin to suffer they see only one aspect of reality. For example, if your child is sick, that is all you think about, and it is hard to remain calm. You feel depressed and you cannot see things from any other perspective. But if you just step back from your problems and try to be objective, you will see that your child is not the only one suffering an illness. The child will recover more quickly if you enjoy peace of mind. You can keep your head in times of trouble by looking at the situation from many perspectives and realizing that many other people have troubles, too.

The disciple Devadatta rebelled against Shakyamuni, the historical Buddha, and even tried to kill him; yet Shakyamuni praised Devadatta as a good friend. Devadatta's acts were wicked, but Shakyamuni taught that if we rise above our hatred of evil and consider it objectively, we will realize how important it is to walk the correct path. If we interpret Devadatta's behavior correctly, it can be a lesson leading to further spiritual growth.

A knife can be used to kill or to perform surgery, that is, for evil or for good. The mind is equally adaptable. We can think wicked thoughts leading to wicked deeds, or good thoughts leading to good deeds.

The world is filled with suffering. In its midst, we must look for meaning in everything and learn from every experience. We must ask ourselves what the Buddha is trying to show us. It is this desire to learn that marks the boundary between enlightenment and delusion.

❦   ❦   ❦

The British historian Arnold Toynbee said that history is a series of challenges and responses. Improving ourselves through exhortation, encouragement, and competition with our fellows is important in making life meaningful. Taking another person's example as a challenge, responding to another's challenge, makes us want to improve ourselves. In all things, it is the repeated cycle of challenge and response that is the cause of progress and development.

Yasuhiro Yamashita broke many records as a judo champion. He often said he welcomed challengers but hoped to keep winning as long as he could. If he were easily defeated, he said, challengers would hardly need to improve themselves. It was that spirit that made him a record breaker, with 203 consecutive wins, and inspired younger athletes in their training.

Engaging in competition should not mean hating your opponents and wanting to destroy them. Rivalry in the best sense means wholehearted effort to equal your opponents and then surpass them. In the traditional martial arts of Japan, training and tournaments have always been important for the way that they encourage continuous effort at self-improvement. Victory or defeat in a match is considered just one event in a long process, not the goal of training.

To develop your potential fully, you need a rival you can train yourself to surpass. When you are satisfied with yourself and have no higher expectations or goals, you stop improving. Some people, of course, give little thought to having a rival, preferring to work quietly and diligently on their own, away from others' gaze. There are indeed many different ways of living, but what is important in all cases is doing your best in whatever you undertake.

People also have many different ways of choosing rivals. A rival does not have to be a living person. Some read biographies of famous people, are moved by their example, and make these people their ideal. For Buddhists, the Buddha is our rival in the true sense of the word. The ultimate aim of our practice is to emulate the Buddha.

The thirteenth-century Japanese Zen priest Dogen said that daily practice itself is enlightenment. He taught that practice and enlightenment are the same thing, that our daily practice, just as it is, is the Buddha's practice.

We should think of everything we do as part of the bodhisattva practice, as the Buddha's practice, and proceed along the Way, taking care to make our practice rich in meaning so that our inner enlightenment is constantly increased.

❧   ❧   ❧

Masahiro Mori, a robotics engineer and general director of the Mukta Research Institute in Tokyo, claims that there are two ways of thinking, the "stock" method and the "flow" method. The stock method of thought holds that experiences are to be saved up and accumulated. Once you have seen or heard something, you know it and there is no need to repeat the learning experience a second or third time. The flow method of thought, in contrast, values the process of arriving at a particular conclusion. Though you may not be able to accomplish a particular thing at present, you will be able to in the future, and it is the process of arriving at that accomplishment that is most valuable.

The stock method is used by people who think a single viewing of an educational film is enough. People who employ the flow method, however, are willing to see such a film again and again, looking for something new in it each time and deepening their understanding of it. Mori relates his own experience of seeing a film on one research project over 160 times and discovering something new in it on each viewing. He suggests that the stock method of thought was predominant in the past but that the flow method is now coming to the fore.

Religious teachings are meant to be understood through the flow method of thought. With repetition, difficult teachings gradually take root in our minds and we begin to understand them. The most valuable aspect of Buddhism is daily religious practice bringing us closer to fulfillment of the Buddha's original vow. For members of the organization to which I belong, this might mean being thankful for birth as a human being and grasping the true purpose of life while engaging in morning and evening devotions, while taking part in *hoza*, or counseling sessions with fellow believers, or while sharing the teachings with nonbelievers and guiding them to the faith.

In our organization, we hear the complaint that the same things are always said in counseling sessions with fellow believers and in sermons. Our religious leaders may be partly to blame, but at the same time it is important for those who would progress spiritually to try to discover something new in what they are hearing, even though they may be hearing it for the second or third time.

In the chapter "Ten Merits" of the Sutra of Innumerable Meanings, the work that introduces the Lotus Sutra, it is written: "This sutra . . . stays at the place where all the bodhisattvas practice." The true value of the teachings of the Lotus Sutra is revealed only by practice.

I think we have all had the experience of finding that we did not actually understand a teaching we had thought we understood after one hearing or reading. Each time this happens, we discover what we misunderstood. We realize we must hear or read the teaching a second time, or as many times as necessary until we think we understand. As long as we have this attitude, even after a hundred hearings or readings we will find something new, become aware of something previously unnoticed.

We would do well to avoid the stock method of thinking, which disdains repetition. Instead, as with the flow method of thinking, we should value the learning process and not waste repeated opportunities. Only with such unceasing effort will our daily religious practice be filled with gratitude, purpose, and vigor.

FINDING SPIRITUAL
SATISFACTION

The ability to be profoundly moved by the things we see, hear, and touch greatly enriches life. Emotional experiences of this kind resound in the mind with a freshness that makes us feel alive. The inability to be moved is one of life's greatest unhappinesses, since it cripples the spiritual activity of beings thought to represent the pinnacle of creation. Without the ability to be moved, a person may as well be dead.

Humankind has largely lost the ability to be touched by the beauty of a flower or to be stirred to admiration by a good deed. And that loss, experienced by most adults, influences the world of children.

The solution lies in having aims in life. Too many people either concern themselves solely with immediate material desires or simply drift through life without aims of any kind. Such people not only lack interest in spiritual matters but also sometimes allow selfish calculations to stimulate them to act against their conscience. As long as life goes on as usual, these people do not run into problems. But hard times and setbacks can cause such people to lose sight of life's meaning and to despair.

When things take a turn for the worse, such people tend to blame circumstances or other people. Laying blame elsewhere neither solves problems nor leads to self-improvement. Many passages in Buddhist scriptures stress our responsibility for our own acts and attitudes.

We often act out of fear of what others might say or out of fear of the consequences of failing to act. But even if the results of our acts are good, we are not likely to get much spiritual satisfaction if we act out of fear.

For example, a child goes shopping for his or her mother out of fear of a scolding, and the child's mother rewards the child with a small coin. Another child goes shopping out of a desire to be helpful. This child's mother, too, rewards her child with a small coin. The second child's satisfaction is much greater. That child knows what joy a good deed brings his or her mother. The mother's joy is the child's joy, and the good deed is the child's greatest reward. All the first child gets is small change. This illustrates the psychological advantage of spontaneous virtue.

All people subconsciously desire to do good and to find happiness in the happiness of others. The fulfillment of this desire brings the deepest possible satisfaction. Choosing service to others as one's highest ideal helps anyone, not just a few special people, discover profoundly moving things every day. People devoted to this ideal see and think about things differently from people without this ideal.

When we are moved by something, we should immediately express our feelings to the people around us, since doing so is certain to awaken a response in them. In a world with so many problems, people of religious faith must have the desire to awaken the capacity for deep emotion in everyone they meet.

❧   ❧   ❧

We often hear our age described as one of diverse values, but a reexamination of events occurring around us suggests that it would be more accurately called an age of confused values. After World War II, most Japanese devoted their energies to satisfying economic and material needs instead of concerning themselves with spiritual matters. Though some people say the present age is one of major interest in religion, confused concentration on material things and money continues to cause social problems.

Many people are unaware that their real motives for doing things stem from subconscious material desires. These subconscious desires cause human beings to spin the dark web of slander, hatred, jealousy, bribery, corruption, anger, conflict, and despair that ceaselessly ensnares society.

Though we need money and material goods to sustain life, they should not be our highest goals.

Nonetheless, the idea that they are worthy goals has a growing influence on education, politics, and other aspects of society. To halt the recurring cycle of social problems in this age of confused values and to restore true humanity, we must put material goods and wealth in their proper places and then reexamine our highest goals in life.

In A.D. 604, as Japan was first attaining national awareness, Prince-Regent Shotoku promulgated his Seventeen-Article Constitution as a guide to government at a time when, just as today, society faced many problems and lacked spiritual unity.

The second article of the constitution states that the Three Treasures of Buddhism should be the mainstay of all people: "Sincerely reverence the Three Treasures. The Three Treasures—the Buddha, the Law, and the monastic order—are the final refuge of the four categories of living creatures and the supreme objects of faith in all countries. What person in what age can fail to reverence this law? Few people are utterly bad. They can be taught to follow it. But if they do not betake themselves to the Three Treasures, how shall their crookedness be made straight?"

We must not allow the three poisons of greed, anger, and folly, which afflict all people, to cause us to despair, for all of us are endowed with the buddha-nature, the potential for attaining buddhahood. If we constantly and diligently devote ourselves to the Three Treasures, we will without fail be awakened to our buddha-nature and therefore do good deeds. Each time I read the Seventeen-

Article Constitution, Prince Shotoku's ideas and words make me realize how deeply he must have wanted to create an ideal country imbued with a profound religious spirit and the teachings of Buddhism and Confucianism.

While faith in the Three Treasures is a requisite for Buddhists, it is also, as Prince Shotoku's text points out, fundamental to living in a way consonant with the best in human nature. Faith in the Three Treasures is of supreme value for our time. We should be grateful for the Buddha's compassion and should live according to his teachings, constantly improving ourselves through contact with others who share our aspirations. Doing these things will enable anyone to find meaning in life and discover true goals.

In times of adversity or confusion, we should never slacken our diligence but should have faith in the Three Treasures and all the more fervently seek the Way of enlightenment. When we adopt this attitude, even hardship and adversity become opportunities for self-improvement and progress.

ầ   ầ   ầ

Reflecting on our thoughts and actions in order to correct our mistakes or our behavior is extremely important. But we must not become obsessed with our past, lest religious faith seem merely a matter of reflection and repentance. We must be especially cautious in this, since people often develop obsessions unwittingly.

In accordance with the principle of cause and effect, we are the sum of our past thoughts and deeds, but the goal of Buddhism is much more than simply to point this out. Buddhism teaches the great importance of the present, which influences the future just as the past has influenced the present. Unless these influences are taken into account, the principle of cause and effect becomes mere fatalism, generating resignation, self-deprecation, and lethargy. These hinder faith from aiding our progress toward the attainment of buddhahood, which is the goal of our faith. We must never forget that reflection and repentance should always be opportunities for further spiritual growth.

Some people try to eliminate undesirable phenomena through reflection and repentance. But this is a mistake, because such elimination neither brings about a basic solution to the problem of the moment nor helps one learn from the phenomena themselves.

Essentially, all phenomena amount to sermons by the Buddha to enlighten us to various truths. In this light, seeming misfortunes like illness, accident, and economic hardship can be viewed as the Buddha's guideposts to more profound, richer spiritual states. Such a view in turn gives us the courage and determination to overcome all hardships and to accept all phenomena with gratitude and joy. People who can do this have made great strides in developing the best in themselves.

Not only do the results of merely reflecting on and repenting of one's past differ from the results of making one's past a guide for spiritual progress, but the difference also grows ever greater with time.

We tend to define happiness and the true merits of faith as avoiding hardship and living in peace. That definition is imperfect, however. Whereas such things as recovering from an illness or overcoming financial difficulties are certainly good in themselves, they are but one kind of merit of faith.

The greatest merits of faith are accepting the compassion of the Buddha in all phenomena with gratitude and joy and adopting this attitude daily in creating a hopeful way of life. Accepting the Buddha's compassion in this way and unflaggingly and resolutely living to share our happiness with others are both our reason for living and the core of our religious faith.

PRACTICING CHARITY

Prosperity has raised people's standard of living, improved their diet, and lengthened their life span. Moreover, prosperity and increased leisure are inspiring in people the wish to make their lives more fulfilling.

Growing numbers of people are finding spiritual fulfillment and meaning in life by participating in volunteer activities related to welfare, culture, education, and the environment. In this trend I sense both the modern unwillingness to find full satisfaction in material wealth alone and the basic human tendency to build communal happiness through mutual caring and assistance.

Serving others sincerely—in Buddhist terms, practicing benevolence, compassion, joy, and impartiality—reveals a purity of heart that seeks no reward. Deep down, everyone has the will to serve others and experiences profound joy and pride when that will is acted on.

Although the spirit of service was perfectly ordinary in the past, as we have grown more affluent and society has become increasingly urbanized, that spirit has tended to fade and emotional bonds between people have been weakened. In these circumstances, charitable volunteer activities are important expressions of all that is good in human nature. Moreover, they not only contribute to the well-being of other people and of society in general but also significantly raise the level of one's own inner life.

Activities in the service of others have far-reaching effects. Children seeing their parents enthusiastically participating in such activities learn about an important part of human life. In this way, the whole family begins to want to serve others. When the number of such families in a community increases, the whole community grows warmer and more harmonious.

True joy and pride arise from serving others actively and voluntarily. Increasing numbers of young people who were raised in material comfort and never experienced serious hardship are now serving as volunteers in developing countries. There they discover worthy human values flourishing despite poverty.

These young people find joy and meaning in their return to fundamental human values. The emotional rewards they reap double their enthusiasm for further service. Indeed, the primary impetus behind service activities is the profound happiness that is the participants' reward, a rich emotion comprehensible only to people who have experienced it.

There are other kinds of joy that are understandable only to people who have experienced them. For instance, a Hindu pilgrim from Calcutta walked for twelve years to reach Mount Kailas in Tibet. Asked why he had undertaken so long a journey, he replied, "So that I'll be happy in the next life." As he spoke, his eyes glowed with the supreme joy of having reached the holy mountain. His was an emotion beyond the comprehension of people who have not experienced it.

As I have said, service brings a similar joy. Allowing young people to participate in volunteer activities instills in them the desire to serve and makes constructive use of their energy. In the present age, in which we strive to emphasize spiritual values and create true abundance in life and society, people of religious faith should take the initiative in cultivating the spirit of service and should begin with practical work close to home.

❦   ❦   ❦

All of us depend on the support, assistance, and goodness of others. Even people who think they are completely self-sufficient live only because of the strength and activities of many people of whom they are unaware. Thus, we do not simply live: we are given life. The Buddhist teaching that nothing has a persisting, independent self means that all beings depend on all others. For this reason, we should humbly recognize our mutual indebtedness, try to be of use to others, and cooperate with one another as we walk along the path leading to true happiness.

There is an old Japanese saying to the effect that kindness is never lost. Though a kindness may seem to have been done for another's sake, it will inevitably stimulate a kindness in return. It is natural to be grateful for a kindness and to want to repay it. Thus it is equally natural to expect that one's good deeds will eventually come home.

But a good deed performed solely in the expectation of receiving repayment is a calculated transaction, not genuine kindness. Those who are not sincere in what they do come to feel bad about themselves and fail to make a good impression on the people they try to help. It is noble to devote one's all to the good of others, but we must always carefully examine our motives to be sure that we expect no repayment for our kindnesses.

True generosity, motivated by the delight of bringing happiness to those we help, is its own reward. Though this motivation seems to deny the self, it is the best means of true self-expression. Sincere service to others revitalizes the server.

Learning to be generous and sympathetic is difficult; it means ridding yourself of selfishness and understanding others' sufferings. Therefore it is very important to experience suffering. If you have never been cold, it is impossible for you to know the pain felt by a person out in the cold. Consequently, those who suffer should avoid becoming obsessed with immediate phenomena—thus losing sight of their larger selves—and should remember that their pain is an important lesson to be faced and mastered. Many people of broad experience have found enlightenment and learned how to live up to the best in human nature through suffering.

We learn from the experiences of our predecessors. Young people should be especially aware that the foundation of their present existence has been passed down to them from others, and they should humbly and earnestly accept and learn what those of greater experience have to teach them.

We should look at our predecessors' experience with renewed respect, for much of what they suffered is unknowable to us today. Being aware of suffering that we ourselves cannot experience is true gratitude.

❧   ❧   ❧

Every Buddhist should strive to be the kind of person who performs charitable acts gladly. The charitable way of life is consonant with the best in human nature. If each person would make a sincere effort to live in this way, the world would be much more pleasant. Making it so is one of the goals of a Buddhist's daily religious activities.

Absorbed in the issues of the moment, many people today tend to be calculating and thus find it hard to be charitable in spirit. When a calculating attitude prevails, warm interpersonal relations break down, and human relations on the job, at home, and in the neighborhood cannot be expected to remain untroubled.

The selfless person who understands the true nature of existence realizes that we all depend on one another and is therefore grateful to everyone. Furthermore, never obsessed by circumstances, such a person responds flexibly to the world's constant change and lives a tranquil, enjoyable life. When able to see still further into truth, such a person senses the wonderful true nature found even in people who seem unpleasant. The daily life of a person who achieves this insight improves steadily. Anyone who rejoices in performing charitable acts for others can attain such insight.

Although the monetary and material giving that comes to mind at the mention of charity is noble and useful to individuals and society, it is not the whole of charity. Easing people's pain by advising them on the path they should follow in life is a form of charity, as is devoting one's physical strength to work that increases others' happiness. Both these kinds of charity are valuable, as are a gentle demeanor and mild speech.

Charity arises from the wish to use one's possessions to bring happiness to others. Anyone can practice charity. Being charitable does not mean abandoning desire. Instead, it means expanding the small self into the greater self. It means not negating but affirming the self.

A youth seated in a subway train, realizing that the elderly person standing before him or her would be as glad of the seat as the youth is, rises so the elderly person can sit. The elderly person's smile makes the youth feel happy and satisfied. In

giving the elderly person a seat, the youth has
learned to rejoice in another's happiness.

Repeated experience of both the joy of performing every charitable act we can and the thankful-
ness for opportunities to perform such acts leads us
along a path of gradual improvement. In this way,
charity gives meaning to life. We should all strive
to experience the emotions that a charitable state
of mind kindles.

ACQUIRING VIRTUE

Fumiya Tsuta—coach of the Ikeda High School baseball team, national champions from the island of Shikoku—sends all freshman players out on the field to pull weeds. He then watches them from behind and, apparently with great accuracy, judges each boy's abilities from the way he goes about this simple chore. Coach Tsuta can read in the boys' backs the signs of all the discipline and education they have undergone at home and at school. His ingenious evaluation system impresses me afresh with the way in which human nature and the home environment are clearly revealed even in the way we do little things.

For people with religious faith, daily discipline consists in guiding others, who observe and judge from behind. Their discipline consists in discovering, refining, and elevating their own virtues. People trust and naturally congregate around virtuous individuals. Individuals of supreme virtue, such as Shakyamuni and his eminent disciples, have immense power to move and influence human beings.

Acquiring such merit is most important in training. Advancing on the path to such merit is a supreme pleasure and happiness.

What I mean here by virtue are the compassion, love, and concern that human beings feel not only for other human beings but for all existence, and which are similar to the process whereby nature creates and nurtures all things. People who ardently desire to create and nurture have this kind of virtue in abundance. People who undertake various disciplines to cultivate that desire accumulate virtue. The effect of such virtue cultivates human beings and makes possible both their accomplishments and the evolution of a warm, creative society.

The Confucian classic *Ta-hsüeh* (Great Learning) includes a statement to the effect that virtue is the trunk and assets are the branches. Often we tend to lose sight of this truth and to mistake the branches for the trunk. For example, assets in the form of capital are considered essential to any business undertaking. People wishing to go into business are willing to borrow to obtain capital, but they must first find lenders. Lenders are unwilling to risk their funds unless they trust in the good faith or virtue of prospective borrowers or of people who are willing to act as their guarantors. In other words, in business, too, assets are the branches emerging from the trunk of virtue.

It requires long years of discipline and many good deeds to acquire virtue. Caring for and loving others to the utmost of one's capacity contribute to the acquisition of virtue. One example of a means of cultivating virtue is participation in Rissho Kosei-kai's program of going without a meal three times each month and donating the money thus saved to a fund for the relief of people suffering from famine in other parts of the world.

Efforts to acquire virtue vitalize and cultivate the individual, bringing an inner light to his or her life. When made repeatedly, compassionately, and unfailingly, such efforts gradually impart virtue. It is my wish that all of us will strive to become people of such great virtue that even viewed from behind, we will be an inspiring example to others.

Thanks to the increasing use of air conditioning, a great many of the world's people no longer suffer as they once did from heat and cold. Nonetheless, the natural rhythms of heat and cold are highly invigorating and stimulate psychological resilience. For this reason, we should think twice before turning on our air conditioners the minute the weather turns hot or cold. Difficult conditions shape and enrich the mind and serve as steppingstones to further development.

Today simply flicking the television switch produces picture and sound instantly. The microwave oven makes hot meals possible in just minutes. But because of excessive reliance on such conveniences, more and more people find delays or difficulties intolerable. Patience is a virtue we should strive to acquire, both to improve the quality of daily life and to enrich our personality. People without patience are willful, disrupt the general concord, and tend to act on impulse.

We should strive to acquire as many virtues as possible in addition to patience, since the acquisition of virtues not only broadens our horizons but also advances us on the path to the attainment of buddhahood. The list of virtues we should aspire to includes wisdom, courage, moderation, justice, introspection, courtesy, discernment, faith, kindness, honesty, and a sense of responsibility.

Ancient Chinese philosophy calls nature (heaven and earth), in the aspect of creator and nurturer of all things, the Way, or *Tao*. The analogous aspect of human beings, which is believed to be an inherent trait inspiring us to love and care compassionately for other humans and all existence just as nature nurtures them, is referred to as virtue.

This belief agrees closely with Buddhist teachings. In Buddhism, compassion is considered to be the force nurturing all things. The Buddha's compassion is supremely noble, but similar compassion is innate in all human beings. Buddhist compassion corresponds to Christian love and Confucian *jen*, or magnanimity, as the source of all virtue.

Improving ourselves constantly for the sake of acquiring the fundamental virtue compassion gives meaning to life. Without letting petty immediate concerns obscure our larger goal and without criticizing others, we should work diligently to acquire the great virtues of nature and the Buddha.

We can begin with small deeds that benefit people close at hand. As such deeds accumulate, seeds of virtue will respond to cultivation and will grow until we become people true to the best in human nature.

❦   ❦   ❦

In surveys of the qualities that young unmarried people in Japan look for in the opposite sex, gentleness ranks highest. But the definition of this quality differs according to the sex of the respondent. The gentleness that Japanese men expect of women consists in warm caring and sensitive consideration, whereas the gentleness that Japanese women seek in men is compounded of magnanimity, occasional sternness, and firm convictions. Thus, to be considered a gentle, likable person, one must know the proper way in which to respond to each person one meets, consonant with that person's personality and the situation.

Superficial charm is ephemeral. To be truly likable, one must represent the best that human nature is capable of. Ancient Chinese thought holds that the best that human nature can achieve is found in the mind that both respects that which is lofty and noble in others and is humble in the knowledge of its own shortcomings. This respect and humility must be augmented by a fitting sense of obligation and modesty.

Society is built on obligations. Each of us is not only obliged to all other beings for the strengths they lend but also responsible for acts that support others. We should therefore always be eager to work for others with humility, free of both pride and sloth.

The common Japanese notion that a sense of obligation is incurred only by the young and inexperienced toward the older and experienced, or by children toward their parents, is wrong. Indeed, demanding that others feel grateful for help or favors only provokes resentment. Parents who wish their children to be grateful must ask themselves if they genuinely deserve gratitude. This kind of modesty can inspire a sense of obligation in others. When parents have this modesty, children are naturally grateful.

Respect, humility, and a sense of obligation stimulate introspection and the desire to improve. Buddhism holds that people can progress or regress rapidly through the ten realms of existence, which range from hell to the realm of buddhas. Human beings live up to the best of their capabilities when they constantly examine their thoughts and actions to avoid low levels of existence, such as hell or the realms of hungry spirits and animals.

To Buddhists—for whom respect, humility, and a sense of obligation are fundamental attitudes— magnanimity and constant concern for others' happiness are important. People who realize this pray constantly that the Buddha will protect the happiness even of those who have temporarily isolated themselves from the teachings. Furthermore, these people unconditionally welcome and rejoice with those who have gone astray when they finally return to Buddhism.

Inability to do these things indicates either imperfect faith in humanity or despair of humanity. We must not despair of humanity but must trust in it wholeheartedly. Instead of demanding things of others, we must strive to find ways to be helpful. Believers who think and act in this way are likable and impart to others the wonderful nature of faith.

BEING TRULY HAPPY

What brings us true happiness? Everyone thinks seriously about this question, and it is a very difficult one, but I think that in the end the answer comes down to being grateful and humble.

For example, you go out without an umbrella and on your way home it starts to rain. Just as you are about to make a dash through the rain, a stranger offers to share his or her umbrella. At such a time, each of us would feel a natural gratitude and thank the stranger for his or her kindness.

Why do we feel grateful? Because we feel that we do not deserve such kindness; a sense of humility, of our unworthiness, comes over us. We could say that humility makes us grateful. It is one of religion's tasks to cultivate in us an attitude that is a combination of gratitude and humility.

We are not born into this world through our own efforts. Our parents are, of course, the direct cause of our birth. If we pursue the matter further, however, we realize that we have received life through the supreme activity of the gods and buddhas, the fundamental power of the universe.

Nevertheless, we tend to think we have come as far as we have in life through our own efforts. As long as we are convinced of that, it is difficult for us to feel humble; but such thinking is shallow and lazy, since it fails to take into account the truth that our existence is sustained not through our own efforts but by the gods and buddhas.

All the material goods and natural riches that sustain us, from food, clothing, and shelter to the air we breathe and the water we drink, lie beyond our control. Once we digest that fact, we cannot help feeling humble and grateful for our existence.

Unless you are grateful to be alive, you cannot be said to be really living. A cafeteria lunch ticket is nothing but a useless scrap of paper unless you know that it can be exchanged for a nutritious meal. In the same way, though you have human form and human capacities, you cannot live fully as a human unless you know the true meaning of life. To know life's true meaning, you must be grateful for life as a gift and a blessing.

We can find true, unshakable happiness in profound contemplation of the role of the gods and buddhas in our lives. We rarely direct our thoughts to the gods and buddhas when things are going well, when we are free from cares and troubles; only when faced with a major problem do we become serious and seek salvation in their teachings. In this case, sufferings are a force for spiritual progress. Through our efforts to triumph over such sufferings, we can cultivate gratitude for the gift of life.

❦   ❦   ❦

We conceive of time only in terms of the present. We call this moment the present; what has already happened is in the past, and what has yet to happen is in the future. Our conception of time is similar to our perception of a boat floating down a river: before it reaches us it is upstream; it draws even with us; then it moves downstream.

But life in fact moves with time's flow. The present moment is gone in an instant, and what was the future becomes the present in the next instant. It is mistaken, then, to try to establish a particular "present" in our lives and view all time from that perspective, dividing it into past, present, and future. If we view the unceasing flow of time from the standpoint of the unceasing flow of our own lives, we will realize that the past was once the present and that the future will soon be the present. We live always in that unceasing flow of the present. Once we understand this, our conception is more like that of a passenger in the boat than a spectator on the shore.

Though we age with the passing years, we want to stay young at heart. We must not worry about distinctions between past, present, and future; instead we must keep fresh our commitment to working to relieve human suffering.

The number of people who consider themselves truly happy is surprisingly small. In general, happiness and unhappiness are relative. Our ideas of happiness are based on comparing our own lives with those of other people.

Suppose someone wanted to go to college but could not and is unhappy about that. As long as this person compares himself or herself with those who did go to college, he or she will always be dissatisfied. But if instead this person thinks of someone who could not even go to high school, the person may think himself or herself fortunate.

As long as they think in relative terms, even people who seem completely free to do as they please are not assured of happiness, since they may compare themselves with people who appear better off rather than worse off.

Yet if we take just one step into the world of faith and study the Buddha's teachings, we learn that although we may have thought we were living through our own efforts, we actually depend on many people. As we look further into the truth, we realize that we are sustained by the gods and buddhas and feel deeply grateful for the gift of life. This feeling of gratitude does not result from comparing ourselves with others; it is a deep emotion that brings us such absolute happiness that we are no longer swept from joy to sorrow by changes in our circumstances.

When we have experienced such happiness, we are grateful for everything—for each day we live, for life itself—and we naturally come to appreciate the value of each day and find true peace of mind.

❦   ❦   ❦

When people look back over their lives, they decide whether things have gone well or not. Whatever they decide, it is very important that they look for the causes of their happiness or unhappiness. Those for whom things did not go well should first ask themselves what was wrong in what they thought or did. Those who are satisfied should take stock of their own efforts through the years and recall just how much they were helped by those around them. When they have identified the causes of their happiness or unhappiness, they should repent what should be repented, correct what needs to be corrected, and then set out again with a fresh resolve to do their best in the future.

We all want our wishes fulfilled; we all want to be happy. But happiness means different things to different people, depending on their spiritual state. Some think they are happiest if everyone in the family is healthy. Others regard business success as the supreme happiness. Of course health and success are possible sources of happiness, but deeper thought shows that the greatest human happiness lies in being alive and knowing the meaning of life.

Buddhism teaches that all human beings have the buddha-nature, that is, that everyone can attain buddhahood. It also teaches that there is no greater privilege than being born human. Unfortunately we usually forget this. Even though we may seem to be aware of it, when something bad happens we blithely blame others, which indicates that we have not really grasped this truth.

The late Haruchika Noguchi, a physician and proponent of holistic medicine, wrote: "The things people make always originate in their minds. Though there is a desk in front of me, it did not exist from the start. It was preceded by thought. If there had been no thought of a completed desk, a desk could never have been made, no matter how much wood was cut. Thought is always foremost. Then come words. If you always follow this order, your wishes will come true and a new world will open before you."

These remarks on the order in which we should act to realize our wishes teach the importance of effort in consummating thoughts, words, and deeds. Noguchi went on to write: "It is important to believe that you already have what you want. Only someone without wealth desires it; only the sick person longs for health. The very words you use to express a wish to be rich, healthy, or happy confirm that you suffer the opposite—poverty, sickness, or sorrow. You are fixing images of these negative things in your mind. Think instead that you are already rich, healthy, and happy and start from there. This is crucial."

I find great freshness and power in Noguchi's words. Our thinking must begin with the belief that we have what we want. Happiness is a matter of self-awareness. Yet happiness is meaningless if it is ours alone. Unless everyone is happy, human wishes are not being fulfilled. If we wish for the happiness of everyone, we are the happier and the greater for it.

The vicissitudes of life give us opportunities to change course. The happiness and sadness we experience open our hearts and minds. With the courageous conviction that we must make even greater efforts, we can face the future. A bright future awaits everyone who adopts this attitude.

MAKING THE MOST
OF OURSELVES

TAKING UP CHALLENGES

Conquering the self is not easy. The thirteenth-century Japanese priest Nichiren had this in mind when he said that we should teach our selves instead of allowing our selves to become our teachers. Teaching the self means overcoming it; allowing it to be our teacher means giving in to it.

Examined closely, overcoming the self can be interpreted to mean showing true love for the self and striving to realize our greatest and deepest wishes. People today are very much concerned with their health and physical well-being. To keep their bodies strong, they make an effort to avoid harmful foods, even those they are fond of. They restrict their intake of alcohol and caffeine. Indeed, without these measures, they cannot hope to achieve good health.

Similarly, triumphing over the self entails keeping a goal in view and exercising self-discipline to attain it. By allowing oneself to be obsessed with the petty desires of the moment, adopt a hedonistic attitude, or flee from difficulties, one loses to the self.

Buddhism teaches that resolving to attain enlightenment is equivalent to actually attaining enlightenment. In other words, making up one's mind to reach a goal is of the utmost importance. Deciding to attain a goal and attaining it are inseparable.

In our modern society with its diverse values, setting goals can be difficult. But as Buddhism teaches, deciding on a goal can greatly alter life's meaning. For instance, we can see that overcoming the self means attaining selflessness. This can be illustrated by some simple comparisons.

Training in kendo, Japanese fencing, demands a kind of self-conquest. Sometimes, however, especially in cold winter weather, fencers have no desire to train. Yet if they neglect practice, they cannot achieve their goals. When kendo practice seems hardest and least appealing, fencers must avoid being obsessed with their own wishes, must overcome self, attain selflessness, and devote themselves wholeheartedly to training. If they do this, they will reach the lofty state of triumph over self.

The *Dhammapada* (Verses on the Law) says that a person who single-handedly conquers a thousand adversaries in a thousand battles but cannot conquer the self is unworthy to be called a victor among victors. Like becoming a hero, overcoming the self demands all one's strength. The enemy in the mind is more fearsome than the enemy in the mountains. As this Buddhist scripture indicates, conquering the self is extremely difficult; however, only by doing so can one make progress in attaining one's ideals and goals.

Endeavoring to realize your greatest and deepest wishes enables you to make the fullest use of your abilities. Any hardships encountered in this effort can be regarded not as difficulties but as reasons for living. People who ardently pursue ideals look neither to the right nor to the left but move diligently ahead toward their goal. Though perhaps difficult to duplicate, this is the attitude we should all strive for. To summarize, it is important first to decide to reach a goal and then, while exercising control to overcome the self, advance toward its achievement.

❦   ❦   ❦

A famous Buddhist teaching says that nothing is permanent, that all things in this world are always changing and coming into and going out of being. Just as the human body changes ceaselessly as its cells die and are replaced, so human existence occurs in a cycle of constant change.

Nonetheless, human beings are conservative and tend to be attached to their accustomed surroundings, in which they wish to live undisturbed. Changes in their setting cause anxiety and fear. It takes great courage and mental preparation to abandon a familiar environment and embark on a new course in life, but resting content with the status quo cannot lead to genuine improvement. We should all strive to take a positive view of life's constant changes and use them as springboards for self-improvement. Doing this gives life true meaning. In other words, we should fully understand and apply in daily life the Buddhist teaching that nothing is permanent.

Despite the many honors the American professional golfer Jack Nicklaus has received and the comfortable life he is able to enjoy, he displays an inspiring determination not to be satisfied with things as they are but always to seek fresh challenges. Cultivating the ardor to break out of established patterns and seek new realms for oneself is extremely important in life. It is all the more important for people devoted to religious faith—people who are enlightened to the great worth of human nature and strive to improve their own personalities and bring about world peace. In all our daily religious training we should diligently aim to cultivate a spirit of ardor.

In the past, a noble personality was valued in Japan, and people cultivated themselves sincerely and studied industriously to attain wisdom. Recently, however, the Japanese seem to have lost sight of that ideal. But we must always bear in mind the great difference that having goals and ideals can make in the meaning of life.

Having firm ideals changes our attitude toward everything—physical and mental discipline, scholarly pursuits, and everyday activities. Having definite goals keeps us young and enables us not only to avoid being disturbed by changes in our environment but also to live each day with enthusiasm and hope.

❧   ❧   ❧

Frequently unwilling to do things that we know are good for us or failing to avoid things that we recognize as harmful, we human beings are reluctant to undertake disagreeable tasks, however much they may contribute to our well-being. But it is impossible to avoid the disagreeable and the painful throughout life. This is why perseverance is indispensable.

Perseverance is one of the practices conducive to enlightenment that Mahayana Buddhists call the Six Perfections. Yet perseverance and the ability to endure hardship seem to be very lightly regarded in this age of high economic growth and material abundance. Nonetheless, we must remember that accepting unpleasant challenges enables us to improve ourselves.

People who feel compelled to do something against their will remain passive, and activities undertaken unwillingly are painful rather than pleasurable. Nonetheless, such activities are not without meaning. For instance, as many undoubtedly know from experience, some people dislike making speeches. When called on to address a group, they do so unwillingly at first, merely out of a sense of obligation. Gradually, however, as they repeat the experience, they become used to making speeches, and eventually they can do so with relative ease.

Instead of avoiding tasks because they are disagreeable, we must address them boldly for their very disagreeableness. We must carry them out despite our reluctance, because making such efforts is important in determining whether we grow as human beings. This is the meaning of discipline.

Because they fear embarrassment and want to show themselves in the best light, young people are especially eager to avoid exposing their inabilities. People who feel this way are able to improve, since they work hard and prepare themselves well to avoid embarrassing themselves.

In difficult situations demanding decisiveness, young and old alike must face their problems with determination to do the best they can. This is why the desire and the effort to avoid being embarrassed or making a poor showing are important to improvement.

Since everything in nature is in flux, human beings must not become set in their ways, refusing tasks at which they have never been skilled or at which they have failed. Yet self-consciousness makes it difficult to achieve this flexibility, inhibits the sincere desire to improve oneself, and can lead to cowardice. Thus it is important to take the first step, no matter whether it may lead to success or failure, no matter whether you are good or bad at the task you undertake. If you should fail, reflect on the causes of your failure and, with the intention of succeeding the next time, start over again.

Remaining content with success ends in no improvement. Human beings do not live for results. We must learn from each mistake and make each success the starting point for further growth. Without fearing the outcome, we must accept difficult challenges and in this way overcome our self-consciousness. We should always be willing to meet the challenge of all the hardship and unpleasantness we encounter in daily life.

REMEDYING
SHORTCOMINGS

According to two proverbs popular in Japan, good medicine tastes bitter and good advice grates on the ear. It can be hard to respond graciously when someone we work with or look to for advice makes us uncomfortable by pointing out our failings. Sometimes we are aware of our shortcomings and the need to correct them; sometimes we are completely unaware. The implication of the proverbs mentioned above is that accepting criticism as an aid to self-discipline fosters rapid spiritual growth.

We are unconscious of our immense reserves of physical strength. In emergencies people can perform unimaginable feats when sudden stress causes glands to flood the bloodstream with adrenaline and other hormones that are normally present in only tiny quantities.

In the same way, provocative exchanges with the people around us, however stressful, can call up mental strength. If we heard only soothing, pleasing comments, we would hardly benefit. Young people would not mature if they heard nothing but praise. Improvement and development depend on heeding and pondering adverse criticism. People who close their minds to criticism, as if it were a nuisance, cease to grow.

Indeed, it is a great blessing to know people who care enough to point out our failings and thus help us develop our full potential.

❧　　❧　　❧

Inexperience and immaturity often spell defeat in carrying out projects or pursuing goals. Young people sometimes become discouraged when they find that a task is beyond them even though they have tried their best. This happens because they lack the experience to recognize that failure is possible in any undertaking.

An excessive fear of failure and an overly cautious approach can sap a person's confidence and make him or her want to give up, forfeiting any chance of success. But if we look for the causes of failure, make the necessary corrections, and try again, success comes within reach. History is a record of trial and error. Despite repeated failures, humanity has produced the great inventions and made the great discoveries that have shaped modern civilization. Failure is the author of success. When we overcome our failures and take them as valuable lessons, they open up new possibilities for us.

No one sets out to fail, but failures occur nonetheless. Perseverance and the lessons of failure help us develop self-confidence. It is especially important that young people not be discouraged by small mistakes and that they adopt a positive, daring outlook. It is by taking mistakes in stride that they will develop into wise adults with a rich store of experience.

❦　　❦　　❦

New employees, fresh out of high school or college, often make mistakes and are reprimanded by their supervisors. Without parental guidance and on their own for the first time, some of them may feel trapped and unhappy. Correction may be hard for them to accept. But young people who accept correction not as a sign of dislike but as on-the-job training to prepare them quickly for greater responsibilities will feel grateful.

Young people who are determined to be useful to society and to improve themselves as much as they can will have the foresight to take criticism in the right spirit and will try to rectify their shortcomings. On the other hand, those interested only in money and comfort may simply be annoyed by criticism.

The historical Buddha, Shakyamuni, said that we live in a world of suffering and that suffering must be endured. In other words, suffering is a part of life and is essential to spiritual development. We improve ourselves by overcoming the many sufferings we encounter in the course of our lives.

The late Haruchika Noguchi, a proponent of holistic medicine, wrote: "What enables a car to move is friction between its tires and the road. . . . A car can barely move on slippery ice because there is too little friction." Suffering relates to personal growth in much the same way that friction does to the motion of a car. It allows forward movement.

The Lotus Sutra, one of the most important scriptures of Mahayana Buddhism, teaches that selfishness is the principal cause of suffering. Our lives are affected greatly by whether we realize this and look within ourselves for the causes of our suffering or try to evade suffering by ignoring its causes and changing our surroundings. Temporary escape is possible, but unless we rid ourselves of selfishness, new surroundings will not save us from further hardship and pain.

Suffering is, ultimately, a source of comfort. Accumulated experience and the ability to accept criticism and advice help us acquire flexibility of mind and self-confidence, and these in turn bring inner peace.

On a television program not long ago, a Buddhist priest said: "Religious discipline and training don't have to be all hardship. They can teach us to find profound spiritual satisfaction in trusting one another and helping one another overcome suffering. This kind of satisfaction is what enables us to go on with our discipline and training."

Obviously people are unlikely to persevere in anything that brings unrelieved suffering. But with perseverance, we can overcome suffering and find happiness. About three years ago I started an exercise regimen. At first my legs and hips ached, but I did not give up. Gradually, as I became used to the exercises, the pain went away and I began to feel that I was in good condition physically. What had begun as a hardship turned into a source of well-being.

Enduring and triumphing over suffering bring pleasure and happiness. This is why we should all strive diligently to progress and should realize that suffering is essential to spiritual growth.

GAINING THROUGH
ADVERSITY

Sermons that Shakyamuni, the historical Buddha, delivered at the end of his forty-five-year teaching ministry are gathered together in the Lotus Sutra. In chapter 16 of this sutra, "Revelation of the [Eternal] Life of the Tathāgata," the Buddha says:

> I, ever knowing all beings,
> Those who walk or walk not in the Way,
> According to the right principles of salvation
> Expound their every Law,
> Ever making this my thought:
> "How shall I cause all the living
> To enter the Way supreme
> And speedily accomplish their buddhahood?"

It is vitally important that all of us remember always that each phenomenon and each person we encounter represents one of the Buddha's means of expounding the Law, his teaching. Unless we do this, the least setback or frustration can cause us to lose faith. Furthermore, without true faith we may miss opportunities to improve ourselves as human beings.

All the phenomena and people we come upon are essential. We may find some situations unpleasant, and we may have to associate with people we would prefer to avoid, but by overcoming unpleasantnesses one by one and taking the experience of hardship and failure to heart, we grow spiritually and can develop affinities for people we previously thought incompatible.

Ordinarily people shy away from disagreeable situations and seek ways to escape them. Eager to justify themselves, they all too readily criticize and find fault with others. But such an attitude can never lead to solutions to problems. It is most important to examine our own thoughts and deeds to discover the underlying causes of problems, and to see in each trying circumstance the Buddha's profoundly compassionate wish to help us improve.

Each phenomenon is simultaneously the result of a cause and a contributory cause of another result. As long as we are obsessed with results, we find it difficult to alter circumstances and move ahead. Moreover, we tend to overlook beneficial phenomena.

For instance, when a child gets poor marks on an examination despite having tried very hard, the child's parents might suspect that he or she has not been studying properly. A mere scolding is apt to discourage the child. While advising the child to change his or her approach to studying, the parents ought to praise the child's efforts and the improvement he or she has made. A child treated this way is inspired to persevere and can use poor marks to stimulate further improvement.

By being humble and conscientious, we can come to understand fully the things that happen to and around us, enabling us to make them contributory causes of our development and improvement. The attainment of such understanding cultivates in us an awareness of the Buddha's great compassion, brings peace of mind, and reveals precious qualities in the people around us that we may not have been aware of earlier. When we achieve this awareness, we become deeply grateful for others' existence and desire to be considerate of them. We should all strive diligently to become generous people who are consistently responsive to the will of the Buddha.

People who are always cheerful and brimming with vitality whatever hardships they encounter have a refreshing influence on everyone around them. Although we all would like to be this kind of person, disappointments and setbacks often frustrate and dishearten us.

Yet even people who always seem vigorous and composed, who seem to live a constantly blessed life, cannot always avoid difficulties and sufferings. The difference between those people and us is that when confronted with trying circumstances, instead of giving in and becoming despondent they make a fresh start by considering other possibilities.

To start afresh—without trying to flee, envying others, becoming discouraged over prospects for the future, or faltering—it is important to resolve our difficulties by trying to identify and analyze the causes of our current suffering. Moreover, we must not try to find momentary consolation by blaming other people or society for our difficulties, but must be prepared to reflect deeply on our own shortcomings. Inner effort of this kind makes it possible to undergo a spiritual transformation.

It is also important to cultivate interest in sports or hobbies in which we can lose ourselves when we feel discouraged. Having a confidant who is willing to admonish us as well as sympathize with us also helps greatly.

On a deeper level, firmly establishing aspirations and beliefs and never losing sight of worthwhile goals are of the utmost importance in enabling us to avoid being overwhelmed by transient phenomena in our environment. To achieve such stability, we must constantly, diligently train and improve ourselves and whenever possible reflect on ourselves in the light of the Buddha's teachings.

Humbly accepting the Buddha's teachings enables us to see that every problem offers an opportunity for the growth and improvement that permit us to approach the human ideal more closely. When we understand this, a mighty energy wells up from the depths of our being, providing a true vitality that instead of failing us at the first sign of trouble abides no matter what befalls us. We should strive to be the kind of person who manifests true vitality that is a lasting source of creative power and action.

❦   ❦   ❦

Some time ago I was deeply impressed by a television program about the experiences of a physician named Hideo Yonezawa, a sincere believer in the Jodo Shin sect of Buddhism. In a long series of letters, Yonezawa patiently explained the Buddha's teachings to the anguished mother of two handicapped children.

This troubled woman's spiritual evolution was characterized by repeated advances toward understanding followed by relapses into grumbling and complaining about her lot. At last, however, her mind was opened to the truth that her handicapped children, instead of being burdens, were the cause of her having acquired the comforting knowledge of the Buddha. Commenting on this woman's experience, Yonezawa said that we must pay dearly for true faith. Of course, he meant that without suffering, people never know truly deep faith.

Undeniably, it is through hardships and suffering that little by little we come to understand the existence of the Buddha and the precious nature of his teachings. Daily sufferings and life's other trials stimulate spiritual development and lead gradually to enlightenment. When forced into a corner, people often demonstrate startling powers and energies that in many instances inspire the blossoming and maturation of great talents.

The average person looks for the easiest way to achieve a life as free of trouble and effort as possible. Certainly nothing seems nicer than a life of tranquillity and security. But settling for a peaceful life cannot foster personal improvement or true spiritual contentment. The person satisfied with a peaceful life may be completely unable to cope with sudden adversities and the suffering they bring.

Suffering comes inevitably if people try to live life to the full, exerting all their might in their undertakings. Instead of running away in the face of suffering, we must accept suffering for the opportunity it gives us to reflect, change our attitudes, and discipline ourselves for further growth.

As the statement that we must pay dearly for true faith indicates, if we want to have faith and to be truly considerate of others, we must rid ourselves of the habit of putting our own interests first and of blaming others or circumstances for our misfortunes. In all things, we must humbly reflect on and repent our own shortcomings and strive to improve ourselves. When we adopt this approach to life, we come to understand that all beings sustain us and contribute to our spiritual progress. This understanding in turn inspires in us profound gratitude for the Buddha's being and his supreme compassion, which are our guides to true faith.

KNOWING OURSELVES

People who thoroughly understand and diligently practice Buddhism invariably influence others in ways exactly suited to the individual and the situation. They can guide others to salvation because their own thinking is unconstrained and is attuned to the needs of the moment. We should examine our actions in daily life to see whether they manifest the power to influence others. Acquiring the ability to influence others by example should be a goal of our discipline.

None of us is perfect. We all have shortsighted aspects and fixed thought patterns. We all tend to allow ourselves to become obsessed with certain things. But such obsessions fetter the mind, preventing the unconstrained thought that changing circumstances demand. Thus we should attempt to discover and eliminate mental baggage that restricts our freedom of thought.

Self-interest and fixed ideas become mental bonds. For instance, we frequently calculate our own advantage or worry about what others will think of our words or actions. We try to impose on other people our own fixed notions of such things as the behavior we consider properly masculine or feminine. We brood so over our failures that we cannot start over again. All these are examples of mental bonds.

Occasionally a wife may be so busy with the children, housework, and other duties that all she can think of is what she considers to be her husband's obligation to help her. Obsessed with such thoughts, she will probably fail to realize that her husband too is very busy. She may express her dissatisfaction in her attitude or in quarrelsome words.

A person obsessed in this way loses sight of the simple truth that when others too are busy, one must bear one's own responsibilities. On the other hand, someone free of such obsession understands others' circumstances and is not only comfortable when busy but also ready to lend others a helping hand when necessary. Warm understanding prevails between husbands and wives who are free of mental bonds in this way.

The restoration of mental freedom must begin with self-reflection, which in turn means keeping our minds flexible and open to other viewpoints.

Since they convey our thoughts, words are extremely important in enabling us to exert the kind of influence the occasion demands. Our speech must be sincere, because neither the most gentle nor the most severe words can produce the desired effect if they are not bolstered by genuine concern for the other person.

Furthermore, our words must be gauged to others' situation and frame of mind. Teaching a first grader lessons designed for a sixth grader can only cause the child to reject the education and lose interest in learning because the material is too difficult. On the other hand, earnestly presenting first-grade material to a sixth grader can only cause the pupil dissatisfaction and frustration.

Salvation is possible only when there is close rapport between the giver of advice and the recipient. Only if the recipient agrees wholeheartedly with the advice given will he or she want to follow it.

My fellow members of Rissho Kosei-kai are all diligent in their daily religious practice so that they can exert a truly liberating influence on others. Assiduously performing devotions, participating in *hoza* counseling, and accepting advice from those with greater experience, we should strive to be always mentally fresh and to have the kind of faith that enables us to guide others to true salvation and happiness.

❧   ❧   ❧

All the events that occur around us bear a close relation to our own state of mind. Consequently, without becoming obsessed with events, we should strive to discover the fundamental causes of phenomena and to perceive our relation to them. This means cultivating the habit of self-reflection. Someone who tries constantly, day after day, to develop this habit will be able to find appropriate solutions to problems and will be able to act and speak correctly on all occasions, thus improving situations immeasurably.

Symbolized by the lotus, which blooms and bears fruit at the same time, the Buddhist teaching that cause and effect are simultaneous and inseparable means that both cause and effect are reflections of an individual's mind and that all future phenomena already belong to the present.

As an example of how attitudes influence cause-and-effect relations, let us suppose that a husband returns home very late and that he did not call to say he would be delayed. The wife who reacts selfishly, thinking only of the time she has spent waiting, will be angry. Her anger will reveal itself in harsh or frosty words, which can have unhappy consequences. Any apology she may manage to wring from her tardy husband under such conditions is certain to be nothing more than lip service.

Pointing out another's faults calmly, in that person's best interest and in the hope that the failings will be remedied, is a good practice. Generally, however, we human beings cannot remain calm in trying situations.

If the wife in our example had thought not about having been kept waiting but about the heavy workload forcing her husband to be late or about the eagerness to get home that prevented his taking time to telephone, the words and attitude with which she greeted him would have been different. From her welcome, her husband would have understood that she believed and trusted him, and he would have apologized sincerely for his tardiness. The good relations established between husband and wife in this way would have a beneficial effect on relations among all the family members.

Since we are imperfect, our minds tend to be fickle. But being able to observe one's own mind calmly, unemotionally, exerts a regulating influence on the phenomena of the future.

We must therefore constantly observe our own mind, reflect on it, and come to understand our reactions under various circumstances.

With this enlightenment, we can begin changing our attitudes so that we become people capable of caring for others and of feeling gratitude. Moreover, we must do our best to point out to people looking for easy solutions the true way to solve problems.

❦   ❦   ❦

It should be our goal to be people who, not dominated by their surroundings or the conditions in which they find themselves, live always looking toward the future and who are therefore an inspiration and an encouragement to those behind them.

Although most people in Japan today have adequate housing and clothing and enough to eat and are therefore free of the sufferings of poverty, many make themselves miserable by drawing disheartening comparisons with neighbors' situations or with their own past condition. For instance, one family feels inferior for not owning a piano when all its neighbors have one. Someone is embarrassed to wear the same clothes all the time while a neighbor always dresses in the latest fashions.

Obsessed with their circumstances, such people are like manic-depressives, whose feelings soar to the skies with a slight good turn in fortune and sink to despair at a small setback. Such people not only suffer themselves but, because of their mercurial moods, also inflict suffering on their families. This state of affairs comes about because these people see only branches and leaves and magnify them out of all proportion. They ignore the trunk and roots that nourish the tree of life. The trunk is morality and ethics, which enable people to live up to the best of which they are capable. The roots are the Buddha, the gods, and our forebears, who together have given us life and who work unceasingly for our improvement.

Someone once told me the story of the late Doyu Ozawa, a Buddhist priest revered by all who knew him as an embodiment of the compassion of Avalokiteshvara, the Bodhisattva Regarder of the Cries of the World. At the age of twenty-five, while a prisoner of war during World War II, Ozawa suffered frostbite so severe that both his legs had to be amputated. While in a hospital after his return to Japan, he was suddenly enlightened to the truth of his plight: "Suffering comes from comparing ourselves with others. I have been born without legs this very day."

In short, Ozawa affirmed his existence as it was at that moment and then, rising above his suffering, set out to create a new life for himself. As he realized, refusing to accept reality and trying to flee reality do not contribute to personal growth or to the solution of our problems.

People of faith should remember that a grateful spirit supplies energy for progress. In the words of the late Haruchika Noguchi, a proponent of holistic medicine: "It is important to believe that you already have what you want. . . . The very words you use to express a wish to be rich, healthy, or happy confirm that you suffer the opposite—poverty, sickness, or sorrow. You are fixing images of these negative things in your mind."

Noguchi's words are true. The craving for health is proof of obsessive concern over illness. The wish to be happy confirms our belief in what we presently perceive as unhappiness. Driven by such cravings and wishes, we cannot attain true health and happiness.

Buddhist scriptures say that it is not easy to be born as a human being and that it is difficult to encounter the teachings of a buddha, a perfectly enlightened being. Born into this world as human beings, we are endowed with great vitality. As believers in the teachings of Buddhism and other religions that expound life's true meaning, supreme happiness is ours. An even greater treasure is the knowledge that everyone born into this world is blessed with the potential to attain buddhahood, that is, to achieve perfect enlightenment. Truly, just as Noguchi says, we already have what we want.

If we keep all this in mind, we will not be distressed by deficiencies in our lives or even by what we perceive as poverty. Instead, we will be able to lead optimistic lives filled with gratitude.

DEVELOPING MENTAL
FLEXIBILITY

In this age of electronic banking, some people tend to concentrate enthusiastically on amassing more and more possessions. Possessions are undeniably important as the material basis of our lives. Thus the interest in acquiring more of them as efficiently as possible is natural. But single-minded devotion to the desire of the moment and the acquisition of belongings leads to the delusion that happiness can be calculated in terms of money, a delusion that can blind us to the most important aspects of our humanity.

To prevent that kind of delusion and the mental agitation it causes, we must understand exactly what is important and assimilate the spirit of the Buddhist teaching of the true basis for satisfaction. The *Dhammapada*, or Verses on the Law, contains the following explanation of the relation between people and wealth: "Various kinds of property and wealth destroy the ignorant people who do not seek the other shore [enlightenment]. By desiring property and wealth, they ruin themselves and others as well."

Although possessions are necessary in life, they can ruin the ignorant person who fails to seek enlightenment. Knowing how to use possessions to good ends determines one's attitude toward them. Someone who consistently pursues philanthropic and altruistic ideals uses wealth beneficially. But for the person who lacks such ideals and is guided by selfish desires alone, the very possession of wealth can spell ruin.

It is fine to have possessions, but happiness is possible without them. The most important things in life are love, respect, trust, and harmony. Though materially poor, anyone who has cultivated these has great spiritual riches.

Amassing intangible wealth of the spirit makes life truly rich and meaningful. Buddhist teachings outline seven kinds of intangible wealth: faith, morality, contrition, fear of doing evil, knowledge of the teachings, giving, and wisdom.

Certainly these seven intangible treasures are rewarding and uplifting; unfortunately, however, people tend to be dissatisfied with the intangible and to prefer concretely calculated material benefits. But as long as they are obsessed with satisfying immediate desires, they cannot attain tranquillity, or unconstrained thought. The Sutra of the Last Teaching (*I-chiao-ching*) says: "One who would escape all suffering must contemplate the meaning of satisfaction. Knowing what satisfaction means brings spiritual riches and tranquillity. One who understands what satisfaction is sleeps peacefully even on the bare ground. One who does not understand it would be dissatisfied even if living in heaven and would be spiritually deprived even if rich. The person who understands satisfaction is rich in spirit."

Possessions are indispensable to everyday life; letting the ideal of wealth of the spirit guide our thoughts and deeds enables us to use possessions to advantage.

❦   ❦   ❦

Athletes prepare themselves psychologically to do their best at crucial moments. The pressure of participating in major competition—which is greater than nonathletes might imagine—often prevents contenders from doing their best. Being able to face keen competition with calm and composure, without nervousness or undue excitement, plays a decisive role in athletic performance. The same calm is necessary in ordinary life.

Becoming too tense or excited narrows our perspective, making it impossible to take a sweeping view of situations and thus distorting our interpretations. This is why our wise forebears insisted that at times of excitement it is vitally important to pause, catch one's breath, and regain composure.

The habit of one broadcast journalist illustrates the importance of a calming pause. Whenever the network gives him an important assignment, after making all necessary preparations to cover the story he goes to the washroom and shaves. This calms him. As he moves the razor slowly over his face, he organizes his thoughts about the assignment.

When we are calm, we avoid obsessions and can make objective, comprehensive assessments of situations. Although the intense pressure of daily activities and work sometimes makes flexibility of mind hard to achieve, such flexibility can change our lives for the better. People who thoroughly understand their own goals and ideals and constantly strive to achieve them have the power to preserve the necessary flexibility. Such people are naturally aware of how to live and enthusiastically pursue their own goals. Laxness in pursuit of their goals, however, may cause people to become obsessed with trivialities. When this happens, they lose sight of life's true meaning and become troubled, confused, and incapable of taking a comprehensive, objective view.

Recently Michio Nagai, a former education minister of Japan, remarked that people today, even if they are materially well off, often suffer from a spiritual poverty that makes them impatient and inconsiderate. Affluence does not necessarily ensure happiness. Indeed, there are many people in the world who, while poor in monetary terms, lead happy, spiritually rich lives. True mental flexibility comes from living always to the best of our abilities and as humanely as we can, with neither impatience nor greed.

Religious faith, especially daily Buddhist training, renews in us the spirit of gratitude for the benefactions we enjoy and helps us achieve flexibility of mind. Flexibility of mind in turn leads to happiness. We should all strive to find time each day to pause and rediscover ourselves and in this way give our lives greater meaning. Rediscovering ourselves contributes to our happiness by giving us flexibility of mind.

Deep emotion is the greatest spur to self-improvement, but it should always be accompanied by careful thought.

A statement in the *Analects* of Confucius urges daily self-reflection with the goal of discovering one's mistakes. Following this excellent advice can play a major role in imparting meaning to one's life. The initial exhortation is followed by three specific subjects for reflection: confirmation of the purity of one's motives in serving others, confirmation that one is being perfectly sincere with friends, and confirmation that one offers to teach others only things that one has mastered oneself.

In other words, instead of hazily recalling the things that happen from day to day, we ought to be specific in our daily self-examination. It is equally important to occasionally examine ourselves more thoroughly and deeply than usual so that we stay on the course of sound development.

Keeping a diary is a good way to organize the mind and analyze thoughts and deeds more deeply.

Expressing ourselves in writing helps us focus our thoughts. Thus a diary must do more than record a string of events: it must also include inner, spiritual matters. No one can keep such a diary for us; we must do it ourselves. Furthermore, the person who rereads a deeply thoughtful diary can trace his or her development as clearly as a physician traces heartbeats on an electrocardiogram.

Because of the fast pace of life today, we are so pressed for time that we risk losing sight of ourselves. Setting aside time for self-reflection not only establishes a refuge in our lives that keeps us from being controlled by the force of habit but also gives us an opportunity to rediscover ourselves. The effect of self-reflection is heightened when the time for reflection is made the time for keeping a diary, as well.

The late theoretical mathematician Kiyoshi Oka said that as long as he was in the habit of doing research, he could begin work the minute he sat at his desk. But if he had been away from his research for a while, his attention wandered. It then took some time before he could lose himself in deep thought. The same problem occurs in keeping a diary: when the habit has been broken, getting started again is difficult.

The opinions of others are an important source of material for self-reflection. Instead of relying solely on our own perceptions, we need to see ourselves as others do. In this connection, family discussions are extremely valuable. For instance, conversation after dinner, when the whole family is together, provides an excellent stimulus for self-reflection and deepens family ties. Of course, not everything said will be pleasing, but even harsh comments deserve to be listened to calmly.

Since flexibility of mind can improve the way we live, we should all strive for mental flexibility and resolve to set aside a definite time each day for self-reflection, renewal, and self-improvement.

LEARNING TO BE TEACHERS

Life is often compared to a journey. Before reaching the end, we must cross smooth and rough patches in both fair weather and foul. We sometimes require walking sticks to help us over difficult stretches and signposts to guide us through passes. The thought and wisdom of our forebears, reinforced by contemplation and actual practice, serve as our walking sticks and guideposts on the journey of life. True happiness is attained by acquiring wisdom, but it cannot be acquired in a day. The acquisition of wisdom demands sincere effort to learn in all aspects of life, the inspiration of ideals, and the unfailing will to improve.

Learning is more than increasing knowledge or understanding things intellectually. To understand a thing with one's head alone is not to have mastered it. Mastery entails understanding with the whole body, which is possible only after we have repeatedly put into practice what we have learned.

The five practices of teachers of the Law set forth

in the Lotus Sutra indicate the importance of practice. The five practices are receiving and keeping the Lotus Sutra, reading it, reciting it, interpreting or explaining it, and copying it. The practical actions of reading, reciting, explaining, and copying the sutra make it possible to master the teachings. And this in turn enables us to receive and keep the sutra with even deeper understanding.

More than merely mastering knowledge or technical skills, true learning includes striving to become the best human being one can, perfecting the self and elevating the personality. The task of learning is often compared to scaling a mountain: the more one learns, the loftier and more distant the summit seems to be.

Probably no one truly believes he or she knows everything and has nothing else to learn, yet people tend to be conceited about their knowledge. Thus it is essential to be sincere about learning, especially when we are young. Mindful of the old saying that lack of effort in youth and the prime of life leads to pain and grief in old age, we must realize it is important to study diligently and enthusiastically while young in order to lay the foundation on which to build a richer later life.

People often have a vague knowledge of a subject, only to discover on being required to explain it to others that they actually do not understand it at all. Of course the degree of one's interest in a subject has a bearing on one's understanding of it. Nonetheless, if one is asked to lecture before a group, instead of shrinking from the task it is better to welcome it as an incentive to study further. Having to explain something to others as well as we can makes us aware of our deficiencies and stimulates us to reflect on the need for additional effort.

People who can explain things so that others understand are usually very experienced at explaining. In addition, they themselves are constantly learning, and discovering and remedying their own deficiencies. In other words, teaching others demands that one learn; and learning qualifies one to teach. To engender wisdom and cultivate a profoundly humane personality, teacher and pupil must learn diligently together.

Both learning and teaching are means of discovering our own deficiencies. Furthermore, teachers must always calmly reflect on their own attitudes and must also make ceaseless efforts to continue learning.

Learning from the past is important because our forebears have left much that is extremely useful to us today. The history of people of the past and of the events they experienced is a reservoir of wisdom and philosophy. This is why learning about history through books, television, and films enables us to look more deeply at our own way of life and in this way make our lives richer and more meaningful. Moreover, history is rich in lessons for people who are suffering or in despair or are about to make a new start in life.

In history we see the rise and fall of civilizations and individuals, the fortunes of people experiencing the full gamut of emotions. From history's vicissitudes, a single pattern emerges. The beginning of a process is always characterized by vigorous creative energy. Then, as the form being created reaches completion, a period of stability follows. Thereafter, under the influence of inertia and apathy, the initial energy is dissipated, people become dejected, and downfall is inevitable. The history of nations and of the careers of people of the past reveals this, and the same pattern is occurring today in our own lives. Caught up in the maelstrom of events, however, we do not perceive the pattern, even when we are about to err. History enables us to understand our own circumstances and the underlying reasons for our mistakes.

The study of history provides us with many guideposts that can help us avoid foolish repetition of past mistakes. Three principles especially stand out among the things I have learned from such study. First, do not become obsessed with proximate phenomena, but always take the longest possible view of affairs. Second, do not become obsessed with one aspect, but always take a broad, multifaceted view of affairs. Third, do not become unduly absorbed in details, but always observe fundamentals. Examining events and considering them deeply in this way enable us to acquire wisdom and formulate guidelines based on experience gleaned from the past.

History is not confined to books. Each of us has

an individual history extending from birth to the present. Our own histories and those of all the people we meet contain many important lessons and much nourishment for our further development.

Among the many things older and more experienced people can teach us is the kind of consideration for others that is gradually disappearing from modern life. Because our society has become increasingly urbanized, most people have no experience with farming and know nothing of the hardships of a farmer's work, and therefore are not thankful enough for their food. This is just one example of the way in which consideration for others has tended to languish as life has become more comfortable.

Through experience and learning from our forebears, we should to try to cultivate consideration for others, since such consideration enriches life and is important in maintaining social harmony. History should not be approached as a subject to be learned by rote, but as a guide to living. If we adopt this approach, we will always comprehend the wisdom that history bequeaths us.

We are diligent in daily religious discipline in order to perfect our character, that is, to become people who are naturally in harmony with the time, the place, and those around them. Such people are always aware of the essential self, even in the face of ceaseless change, and they try to improve not only themselves and those around them but also their surroundings. We can become such ideal people only through earnest efforts to master the principles of right living, advancing step by step.

In mastering the principles of kendo, or Japanese fencing, there are three stages of progress. The first is sticking to the principles, and the second is deviating from the principles. But since merely deviating from the principles can lead to recklessness and injury, trainees must proceed to the third stage, that of transcending the principles. At this stage, they have reached a higher level, where they are free to be creative and original, suiting their technique to time, place, and opponent, while never forgetting the principles.

We experience similar stages in perfecting the personality. First we must study and master the principles of right living. After this we are free to make full use of our own abilities. Repeated efforts to master the principles of right living ultimately enable us to react appropriately in all circumstances without ever losing sight of the essential self.

Although various stages precede the attainment of the ability to react in this way, the most important is mastery of the principles of right living. Learning the principles of right living means first of all sincerely accepting and following the advice of more experienced people and of leaders. Next, it is important to be always ready to examine and master the import of traditional wisdom implicit in such principles. It is of course desirable that people at this stage of learning be supported by older people of greater experience and development.

Since ancient times the Chinese have considered the well-rounded person to be one whose personality combines the gentle warmth of spring, the fervent enthusiasm of summer, and the severity of autumn and winter. Such a person will sometimes embrace younger people with warmth and will sometimes guide them with severity, and will always be ardently oriented toward the achievement of ideals. With the aid of the stern love of such a person, younger people can develop wholesomely and can cultivate in themselves the essential virtues. Furthermore, outstanding older people set examples that inspire younger people to further self-improvement. In short, leaders and people of greater experience exert a very strong influence on young people.

BUILDING HARMONY

BRINGING OUT THE BEST
IN OTHERS

The way we use words can either encourage and inspire or discourage others. Kindness and consideration expressed in ordinary conversation are encouraging and are a source of great happiness if they inspire fortitude and hope for the future. Callous words hurt and discourage. This is why we should always be careful to use right speech, words that are appropriate. With the aim of encouraging one another and creating harmonious relationships, we should think carefully about everything we say.

Speech is said to be what distinguishes human beings from other animals, both accounting for our spiritual evolution and making it possible for us to develop further. We use words in thought, speech, and writing. Right speech not only improves and elevates us but also brings out the best in the people we meet.

Emphasizing the importance of right speech, Buddhism teaches that a serene countenance and loving words are required in guiding and teaching others. Truly loving words arise from a warm, compassionate heart. The words of people who sincerely care for others as much as they care for themselves always impress us. These people can lead others to salvation.

Sometimes we are tempted to blurt out comments inspired by the emotion or self-interest of the moment. At such times we should take a deep breath and pause to reflect on how it would feel to be the butt of such remarks. If we pause to consider others' feelings, we can think of the right thing to say. For instance, the way we comment on food prepared for us can express gratitude or imply criticism. Compare "That was spicy, and very good" with "That was good, but rather spicy."

It is important to remember that words rebound on the speaker like a ball thrown against a wall. It is said that constantly finding fault with others mars the face of the faultfinder. Harsh criticism can stimulate another person to self-reflection and improvement only if he or she recognizes that the criticism is warranted. Criticism inspired by self-interest or bias can only invite denial.

Since words reflect the inner personality, we should strive to be the kind of profoundly humane people whose speech—together with fitting acts and trustworthiness—has the power to influence others for the better.

As children in Suganuma, Niigata Prefecture, one of my younger brothers and I often helped in the farm work by weeding sweet-potato patches in the blazing summer heat. When exhausted, we would sprawl between the rows of potatoes. Although my brother suffered heatstroke once, most of our memories of those times are pleasant.

As we grew older, we were permitted to take on more challenging tasks. The work we did was not very important, yet we were happy to do it and now recall it with pleasure. For instance, one year at planting time we were allowed to do nothing but throw bundles of rice seedlings down to people working in the paddies, but the following year we were proud and gratified to be permitted to take part in the actual planting. Such permission meant that our ability to do more demanding work was being recognized.

We all have unique traits and strengths and weaknesses, and all of us—even if only subconsciously—want our talents recognized. Realizing that we are all alike in this, we should try to guide the desire for recognition in worthy directions. When well bestowed, recognition is welcomed and can be both a stimulus for improvement and a reason for living.

First, we must realize that, having been granted the gift of life, everyone has a role to play and that everyone who has the will and makes the effort can use his or her talents to perform his or her role. If people do not use their talents, there is a problem or they lack something.

Second, it is vital to try always to see others as they really are. This is not easy, because our vision is clouded by emotion, prejudice, lies, conjecture, and calculation of profit. Often we speak and act rashly, unaware of how difficult it is to see others as they are. Thus it is important to question our own state of mind at each moment.

Far from consisting merely of praise or indulgence, friendly advice sometimes requires the pointing out of shortcomings. If the criticism is just, the person being criticized will want to improve. This is yet another reason to remain calm always, trying to see others as they are and trying to make all our words and deeds worthwhile.

❦   ❦   ❦

As instances of right speech, polite greetings are especially significant in establishing harmonious social relations. Polite greetings on first meeting someone make a good impression and contribute to smooth relations. But such greetings must be sincere. If we regard them as mere form, we will greet people only when we feel like it.

Greetings are essentially expressions of trust and respect. In Buddhist terms, they amount to paying reverence to the buddha-nature, the potential for attaining buddhahood, that is inherent in all of us. Reciprocity is the true import of courtesy: I respect you, and you respect me.

Differences in likes and dislikes color many

people's relationships. Sometimes differences in preferences cause friction between people, but their relations still provide opportunities for broadening and developing the personality. On the other hand, people who cannot accept such differences will never get along with others and will thus hinder their own improvement.

Bias, prejudice, and inflexibility are major causes of social disharmony. We all have faults; no one is perfect. The less magnanimous we are, the more prejudiced we are. Becoming magnanimous enriches us. The more magnanimous we are, the more we can help others be their best.

When we associate with those people we do not especially care for, they may be inspired to work harder at self-improvement if we have the magnanimity to recognize their strong points. And perhaps our magnanimity will help some people become less withdrawn. In other words, recognition can enable people to make the best use of their abilities. Nothing is completely good or evil. Improving one aspect of someone's personality makes him or her a better person. Slightly improving yet another aspect may make that person admirable.

Whether someone makes the best use of his or her abilities and whether we get along with that person both depend on our approach. Keeping this firmly in mind, we should try to broaden and enrich our social relations and make them the starting point for exploring new possibilities for our-

selves and others. When we venture into new fields
or environments, we must remember that true
peace is grounded in genuine affection and trust
and in reverence for the buddha-nature inherent
in everyone.

UNDERSTANDING
OTHERS

We find that people's unexpected acts of consideration are heartening and refreshing. Such acts inspire in others gratitude, respect, and a desire to be like the people who perform them. To inspire others, we should all strive constantly to improve ourselves and to be warm and generous.

Keiko Higuchi, a well-known commentator on women's issues, writes of two brothers who lived with her family immediately after World War II. One day her mother mentioned how well brought up the boys were. She gave the example of their ready, courteous acceptance of her unthinking invitation to bathe even though they had presumably bathed earlier that day, while visiting relatives. After their bath they commented on how refreshed they felt. The boys were willing to go to the trouble of undressing and bathing again rather than reject a kindness. Both Higuchi and her mother were impressed by the way the boys put respect for hospitality ahead of the perfectly normal desire to avoid taking two baths in a short time.

Such seemingly unimportant consideration heartens the people who notice it and fosters pleasant social relations. Unfortunately, however, few people today are that considerate, since they are selfishly preoccupied with their own day-to-day affairs.

Certainly one cause of insensitivity is the lack of an environment that encourages thoughtfulness. For example, because of modern transportation, we no longer consider the distance a visitor must come to call on us. In the past, when walking was a common way to travel, distance was a matter of great concern. Now we are seldom grateful for the distance people travel for our sake. In times like these, then, it is all the more important to strive to put ourselves in the other person's place to understand what he or she thinks and feels.

Another factor complicating social relations is the tendency to stress information and knowledge so much that people's feelings are overlooked. For example, assume that a small child runs home excitedly to tell his or her parents of a gleaming golden fish the child has discovered in a nearby pond. Forgetting children's sense of wonder, the parent may belittle the child for not knowing a goldfish when he or she sees one and may lecture the child on their varieties. The child will hardly be satisfied; the child cares nothing about the various kinds of goldfish. In instances of this kind, imparting knowledge is of secondary importance. The vital thing is to share the child's excitement. A truly caring parent will share the joy of discovery, show surprise, and perhaps offer to join an expedition to examine the fish.

When associating with adults, too, we should always try eagerly to be aware of other people's ways of thinking so that we can understand their thoughts and feelings. To this end, we must constantly try to change our narrow, self-centered views, purify our minds, and cultivate in ourselves the generosity to put others' feelings first. Daily effort and consideration of this kind build a cheerful, hospitable society and a meaningful life.

❦   ❦   ❦

For the sake of fellowship, happiness, and deep spiritual fulfillment, it is essential that we try to understand others. We must tune in to others' frequencies or channels, just as we tune a radio or a television set to receive a broadcast.

Understanding begins with attentive listening. Often people are too preoccupied with themselves to understand what is being said to them. One cause of this preoccupation is selfishness. Self-centered people interrupt others to express or impose their own ideas. Some people, while seeming to listen, are in fact so lost in the jumble of their own concerns that they understand nothing at all. Prejudices also hinder understanding. Although prejudiced people may appear to listen, mentally they are stopping their ears.

To become better listeners, we need constantly to reflect on our shortcomings and improve our attitude through religious discipline. A marked improvement in attitude can take a long time, and we should not be discouraged by our failings along the way. All we can do is try to make as much progress as we can each day. Furthermore, we must learn not to be self-centered when we talk with others. Once we have learned this, we will not only understand what others say but also penetrate to their innermost thoughts.

Some people simply want to be heard. Some are too overcome by their suffering to see that the answer they seek is in the very words they themselves utter. Others bring unhappiness on themselves through selfishness. But once we can sense people's thoughts from their conversation, we learn naturally how best to relate to them.

Sensing others' thoughts in this way is relatively easy for experienced people, but the inexperienced need not be discouraged to try. As is written in the great Confucian text *Ta-hsüeh* (Great Learning), "If you seek sincerely, though you may not hit the mark you will not be far off." Thus the task of understanding other people is not impossible if you go about it diligently and sincerely.

For instance, instead of immediately and flatly denying a child's request, parents should try to discover what lies behind it. Why are new toys or other playthings so important? After starting a dialogue with a question like "Must you have it right now?" or "Would something else do just as well?"

parents can explain their own views with the likeli-hood of being understood. Obviously, parents must sometimes sternly refuse a child's request. None-theless, an exchange of this kind is convincing to children even though they may not get their way.

To too many parents, their children's demands are a nuisance. When this is the case, parents and children fail to agree because their ways of thinking differ. This lack of agreement results in a feeling of being misunderstood that can sadden children and exert an undesirable influence.

The world changes every day. People become busier, and there are always new ideas. Under these circumstances, it becomes increasingly difficult to remain calm and to understand what others think. But it is precisely because we live in such a changeable world that we must strive all the harder to enhance mental and spiritual contacts and com-munication. The fruit of our striving can become the foundation for a truly humane society based on mutual trust and concern.

As a guide in training ourselves to be people who are like receivers tuned to others' sufferings and in-terests, we can turn to Avalokiteshvara, the Bo-dhisattva Regarder of the Cries of the World. To tune ourselves to other people's frequencies, we need to elevate ourselves to a high enough spiritual plane to be able to respond appropriately to their feelings. We must also keep ourselves free of bias,

selfish desires, and attachments, all of which inter-
fere with reception of what others say.

Besides being an excellent receiver of the signals
of distress sent out by sentient beings, the Bodhisattva Regarder of the Cries of the World is a
transmitter, too, in that he extends them a helping
hand. He is a kind of transceiver, receiving word of
suffering and, through acts of compassion, trans-
mitting assistance.

Action is essential to the furtherance of the Buddha's work. But not just any action is satisfactory.
Before acting, we must enter a meditative state in
which we can see and understand others.

Attaining a state in which the mind is clear and
receptive demands good physical health because
mind and body are inseparable. It also requires the
feeling of repose that is associated with sitting. We
often acknowledge the need for the repose of sitting. In Japan the formal sitting posture is believed
to produce a sense of repose. And many people
have experienced the calm of seated meditation
(zazen); the stability and calm of sitting in the so-
called lotus position are conducive to good physical
health. Statues of buddhas in this posture suggest
the wisdom and compassion of beings deep in
meditation. When time permits, we should all sit in
the lotus position and calm our minds to provide a
firm foundation for action.

Only in a state of physical and mental selflessness and receptivity can we observe the great vow
of the Bodhisattva Regarder of the Cries of the
World, showing compassion for others' suffering

and considering it our own. In that state, when we try to help people through talking with them, meditating on their salvation, we are of one mind with Regarder of the Cries of the World. We are then tuned in to others' thoughts, and both reception and transmission are accurate.

Consequently, it is most important that we not only resolve to emulate bodhisattvas, exemplars of compassion, but also carry out that resolve. With that resolve as the foundation of our lives, the profoundly compassionate Regarder of the Cries of the World will never be far from us. Instead of relying on his power, however, we must be aware of the need to strive to be like him on our own and must manifest the spirit of this awareness in our daily interaction with other people.

BEING CONSIDERATE

Since differences in personality, background, and philosophy inevitably keep people apart, knowing how and when to approach someone can be difficult. For instance, some young people avoid older people because they think there is a generation gap and that the elderly are rigid in their attitudes. Many of the elderly, meanwhile, refuse to have anything to do with the young, claiming they are impossible to understand.

The two groups keep such a distance from each other that opportunities for contact are hard to come by. This is a great loss for both groups, since it does not allow the young to benefit from the wisdom and experience of the old and keeps the old from being stimulated by the fresh ideas and flexibility of the young. Little creativity and progress can result if people associate only with others like themselves, with whom they agree on everything.

Love and respect are needed for smooth relations between young and old. When both the young and the old love and respect one another, flexible relations based on mutual respect and exchange of ideas become possible. Love and respect are equally important between parent and child, teacher and pupil, and friends. Warm relationships are possible when a sincere regard for others—the very meaning of love and respect—is central to our thinking.

The *Li-chi* (The Record of Rites), one of the Five Classics of Chinese literature, says that the relationships of the virtuous are as fresh as water and their friendship is unchanging. This means that true friendship never changes and is a powerful bond.

Human relations are not necessarily strengthened, however, by familiarity. Indeed, we tend to become overly aware of the failings of people we are with all the time. Consideration for others is most important. Whether or not people are close to us, we can communicate with them from the heart as long as we are considerate.

In 1986 I traveled to South Korea for the first time. In Seoul and a few other cities, I saw for myself the strength of the Confucian tradition in that country. Parents and the elderly are respected, and strict observation of seniority is the foundation of society. Firm adherence to morality and manners is reflected in the almost complete absence of litter and graffiti from city streets. Japan also inherited and long honored the Confucian tradition. But after World War II, with the new insistence on individual rights, the important spirit of respect for parents and elders and of consideration for the young and inexperienced was unfortunately lost.

A passage in the *Analects* of Confucius says that without respect human beings are no different from other animals. The implication is that true harmony is possible in society only as long as we are all imbued with the spirit of mutual respect. Egotism and indifference to other people's feelings frequently lead to clashes that spoil relationships.

Overcoming egotism and indifference to others, and thus easing relationships, requires the modesty to give others the benefit of the doubt whenever there is a misunderstanding. Moreover, a modest attitude is important to the preservation of harmony in the world as a whole. By cultivating respect for our parents, who gave us life and reared us; for our elders, who have amassed experience and wisdom; and for brothers, sisters, friends, and associates, we can help preserve order in the world and contribute to the creation of universal harmony.

Egotism, or self-centeredness, is the opposite of consideration for others. In the workplace, when superiors and subordinates have similar ideas, a generous superior is willing to learn from a subordinate. It is not always necessary for subordinates to defer to their superiors. Superiors should always make the best use of subordinates' talents by respecting their views, but without allowing subordinates to become conceited.

Sometimes agreement between superiors and their subordinates is impossible. When this is the case, we must recognize what is important and not be carried away by personal desires or concern for our reputation. To avoid being carried away, we must not rely on our own experience alone but must constantly seek more information and try to learn from the wisdom of the sages of the past.

Nonetheless, as one saying has it, not everything that goes smoothly goes well, and not all collisions are bad. In other words, even though harmony is important, people must not allow themselves to become obsessed with trying to make things go smoothly lest they become afraid of failure and challenge. The British historian Arnold Toynbee interpreted history as a series of challenges and responses. For the sake of progress a clash, or challenge, is necessary from time to time if we are to help one another improve.

The spirit of harmony and consideration is demonstrated in the Lotus Sutra by the story of the Bodhisattva Never Despise, who reverenced the buddha-nature, the potential for buddhahood, in everyone he met. With that spirit, it is possible to build a society of harmony and love.

❦   ❦   ❦

With some 90 percent of its citizens identifying themselves as middle class, Japan today enjoys an unprecedented sense of prosperity. Material well-being, however, does not always bring spiritual fulfillment. More and more Japanese yearn for a rich spiritual life, recognizing that spiritual values are more important than material possessions. But a truly spiritually oriented society is still far in the future, as is vividly indicated by the growing number of broken homes.

A divorce is granted in Japan roughly every three minutes. In addition, an increasing number of estranged couples continue living together. This arrangement is especially worrisome, since it is common not only among the middle-aged and the elderly but also among young nuclear families.

Founded on love and trust, marriage should be the cooperative effort of two people to build a home and create a new life together. Since the partners usually come from different environments, it is only natural that they have different attitudes and values. For the sake of a happy future, the betrothed should talk things over sincerely until they understand each other and, if possible, arrive at a common approach to their new life.

Wedding receptions in Japan become more ostentatious each year. It worries me that as people focus on the receptions, the wedding ceremony itself— sealing one of the most significant of all human contracts—is becoming a mere formality, and its true meaning and spirit seem to be no longer well understood.

Wedding vows ought to carry over into married life. Each spouse should strive to fulfill his or her proper role so as really to be a lifelong "better half." People's image of the ideal family life differs but usually includes children, prosperity, warmth, and affection. As newlyweds cross the threshold of their new home, they are no doubt filled with hope and joy. But after the first freshness passes, they may cease to love each other and may forget their wedding vows. When worst comes to worst, each spouse wants only to have his or her own way.

The Chinese classics teach that courtesy is an aspect of love. The secret to a harmonious and happy marriage, therefore, is mutual respect.

Married life can be made difficult by any number of problems: hurt feelings, clashes with in-laws, disagreements over a child's education, and so on. Such problems are aggravated when one partner adopts a narrow, selfish view, insisting that the other is wrong. But if the spouses respect each other, they can discuss problems calmly and rationally and admit their mistakes. When crises arise in their marriage, husband and wife need to remember their wedding vows and remind themselves that courtesy is an aspect of love.

GUIDING THE YOUNG

In Japan, recent growth of interest in religion is prompting people to speak of a "religious boom" or a "new age of religion." For both young people and people of mature years, the present turning to religion for help takes the form of fascination with mysticism, fortunetelling, psychics, and miracle workers—an indication of the insecurity people feel in their lives.

Young people look for salvation through the agency of some supernatural force rather than through their own efforts. The present state of affairs is reminiscent of the conditions prevailing in Japan during the Kamakura period (1185–1336), when many people seeking salvation turned to the teachings of the Buddhist priests Nichiren, who advocated chanting the *daimoku*—that is, proclaiming one's faith in the Lotus Sutra—as a meritorious practice, and Shinran, who taught the merits obtained from the *nembutsu*, or chanting the name of the buddha Amitabha.

The wish that deities, buddhas, or exceptionally gifted people would use their great powers to bring people happiness is natural and common and has its own meaning and importance. Nonetheless, few religious believers, least of all Buddhists, expect deities or superior humans to guarantee their happiness.

Buddhism incorporates four basic elements—doctrine, practical action, faith, and proof—and relies on the mind for wisdom and the body for action. Thinking deeply about and practicing the teachings of Buddhism are what guide people to salvation. If we fail to analyze our thoughts and acts and merely hope for deliverance through mystical or psychical powers, we will not appreciate religion's salutary nature.

Chanting the *daimoku* and invoking Amitabha are devices employed by two great religious leaders at a time when abstruse Buddhist philosophy must have been incomprehensible to most people. Furthermore, the *daimoku* and the *nembutsu* express the essence of Buddhism and represent profound faith.

It is the nature of religions to explain all things in the universe and teach people how best to live and relate to one another. Religious teachings help people in the depths of suffering improve their thinking and behavior, showing them that the way to enlightenment and happiness is through diligent self-improvement in the light of those teachings. Mysterious external powers may bring temporary peace of mind, but as Buddhism teaches, a firm foundation of spiritual improvement and stability is necessary for salvation.

Insecurity and suffering are always with us. Shakyamuni, the historical Buddha, observed the social disorder around him and saw that people were striving desperately to escape from suffering. He sought deliverance from suffering through religious discipline. Eventually he was enlightened to the means of attaining true relief from sorrow.

I think causes of anxiety are probably more numerous now than in Shakyamuni's time. We are deluged with more information than we can assimilate and are worried by such threats to peace and well-being as nuclear weapons and environmental pollution. Young people who feel helpless in the face of their problems experience a deep longing for a great saving power, and thus many of them turn to religion for the mystical help they crave.

The nature of our times makes it extremely important for those guiding the young, especially parents, to study religious truth sincerely, practice what they learn, and have firm faith so that they can offer young people the right kind of guidance. Because of their superior receptivity, young people learn very quickly if they clearly understand the fundamentals. They are certain to build hopeful, active, creative lives if they have adult models who, firm in a faith filled with happiness and gratitude, put their faith into practice.

Jiun Onko (1718–1804), a noted Sanskrit scholar and priest of the Shingon sect of Buddhism, concisely described the fundamental attitude required for helping young people grow spiritually and mature: "First show them how to do a thing by doing it yourself. Then explain the task in words and have them perform it. But if you do not praise their efforts, they will not grow and mature."

To help young people mature, it is necessary to set them good examples. They develop by observing and imitating parents and elders, who should explain a task clearly to them and let them try doing it repeatedly. With repetition, the young learn valuable lessons and make progress.

Even after demonstration, explanation, and repeated trials, however, they are still likely to make mistakes, since they may not have understood everything. But criticizing them at this stage is inadvisable, since that might discourage them, stifling their potential and crushing their initiative. Thus praise is important. However discouraged they may be, the young are usually willing to make another try after a little praise.

Jiun no doubt meant that repetition of all the steps in the educational process best helps the young develop and mature. Unlike modern education, which tends to overemphasize intellectual training, Jiun's formative process develops character and a humane personality.

Education cannot develop nonexistent capabilities; it is meant to stimulate those that do exist. Young people, although psychologically immature, have great potential. Helping them develop it requires a parental affection combined with the compassion described by Jiun, as well as the generosity to praise their good points even when scolding seems in order.

The right conditions are needed for sound development. A tree grows well when it has fertile soil, water, and the proper amount of sunlight. Young people's potential can be realized when their ability to learn is developed through the compassion of their instructors.

The ordering of teachings in the Lotus Sutra may also be the sequence best suited for the instruction of young people. The first chapter of the sutra is a dialogue between the bodhisattvas Maitreya, known for compassion, and Manjushri, known for wisdom. The final chapter deals with Universal Virtue, known for practice of the Buddha's teachings. Thus the Lotus Sutra proceeds from the practice of compassion to the seeking of wisdom and finally to the finding of supreme happiness through understanding the nature of all things.

In educating the young, it is extremely important to begin by teaching them with compassion. Compassion is the source of the wisdom instructors need to overcome all obstacles in the guiding of youth.

❧   ❧   ❧

Although people generally choose the quickest, most efficient path to a goal, we should remember that some tasks must be addressed slowly and painstakingly. Parents and teachers should avoid haste and always take a comprehensive view of things.

Some knowledge should be imparted at an early age—including such fundamentals of social harmony as consideration for others, proper greetings, table manners, and courteous speech. Since these fundamentals are basic to our daily lives, they should be taught correctly at the appropriate stage in a child's psychological development.

I would like to comment on three points in teaching young people proper behavior. First, it is necessary to know when and where to correct faults. Sometimes it is necessary to correct a fault immediately. If those responsible for education allow themselves to cling to anger over young people's continual serious misbehavior but fail to correct the young people when the time and place are right, that anger may keep them from getting along well with their charges. Further, their continuing anger may be ignited by even minor instances of misbehavior.

Second, intimacy should not lead to excessive severity. It is easy to reprimand those close to us, but we must realize that intimacy can intensify the shock of reproof. In other words, married couples, parents, and children must respect one another's feelings and be courteous to one another. It is difficult but important to remember that even intimately related people must be courteous toward one another.

Third, it is vital to realize that words are not the

only means of education. Example plays a great role. Observing the behavior of their parents and elders, young people naturally emulate them.

Thorough, patient training develops people who exemplify the best of which human nature is capable: people who are moved by beauty, greatness, and nobility, who strive passionately to attain their ideals, and who are sympathetic to all living creatures. We must believe that all human beings possess lofty qualities that must be revealed and developed.

Correction must not be mere punishment but must always reflect high ideals and the belief that the people being corrected can learn from their mistakes. Great patience may be necessary. As the old proverb has it, the longest way round is the shortest way home.

People are adept and inept at different things and mature at different rates. In educating others we must always recognize these differences, clearly discern what can be taught at once and what requires more time, and always suit teaching and correction to the person, time, and place.

RAISING CHILDREN

A recent study of child rearing in Japan published by the Ministry of Health and Welfare reported that some 60 percent of fathers and 70 percent of mothers had doubts about the best way to raise their children. Some of the issues that concerned parents were their children's educational progress, general behavior, health, friends, mental and physical development (slowness in learning to speak, for instance), delinquency, truancy, and sexual conduct. Asked what would give them the greatest confidence in raising their children, most fathers indicated frequent contact with them and most mothers indicated the cooperation of other family members.

In an increasing number of households both parents work outside the home, drastically reducing the time they and their children spend together, with the result that parents and children grow apart. In this context, the government's study seems to raise anew the issue of the importance of family ties.

When we think about how to raise children, the first consideration should be the parents' daily behavior. Recently the number of mothers working outside the home has increased, but the mother is still central to a child's upbringing. It has been said that 70 percent to 80 percent of a child's character is formed at home. If this is true, a mother's absence has immeasurable impact on a child's development.

No doubt there are compelling reasons for a mother to work outside the home, but in deciding whether to do so her basic criterion should be, what is important in life? Unless she uses this criterion, she will have no educational aims for her children and will be unable to help plan her family's future. Is it more important to enjoy a high standard of living, or should a degree of financial security be sacrificed for the sake of the children's upbringing? With the growth of consumerism and the tendency to believe that money buys pleasure, it is time for parents to reflect and reconsider whether their choice will bring their family happiness.

The cornerstone of children's upbringing should be the mother's gratitude and respect for the father's social position and her moral support of him. Nowadays, children rarely see their fathers at work, as they did in earlier times. A mother should explain and help children understand what their father feels as he works hard for the sake of his family. She should not criticize him if he lies about the house on his days off, resting from his labors. Instead she should make sure the children understand how hard he works and why he needs to rest.

The business world has been likened to a pack of wolves fighting over a rabbit. A mother's duty is to teach her children that earning a living is no easy thing and that their father patiently bears the hardship in order to support the family. The father, in turn, must pour his lifeblood into his work.

At the same time, the wife should stay home and do a good job raising the children and remain always sensitive to her husband's feelings. Cooperation between husband and wife, who thus demonstrate their unique abilities as men and women, ensures that their children will enjoy a wholesome upbringing.

In Japan it is said that a father should not raise his voice to his children more than three times in his life. Of course a father must take a firm stand on important things, but he should refrain from complaining about little things and should encourage his children when they do well. A mother must understand this and always remind the children that even if their father does not say anything, he is always concerned about them. To achieve this kind of perfect coordination, husband and wife should discuss family matters daily.

Raising children educates parents, in a lifelong educational process. Raising children is also a form of religious practice. Sometimes a mother must work outside the home for economic reasons. In this case, she must find ways to make the most of her time with the children. In any event, parents must have firm convictions on the way to live their lives and be models for their children, behaving in such a way that they inspire their children and are a good influence on them.

     ❦   ❦   ❦

Children mirror their parents. Though it may not be obvious, children observe parents attentively and imitate their words and deeds. Parents are their children's closest and most influential teachers. Since parents' ways of thinking and behaving directly affect those of their children, parents can be the best or worst of teachers, depending on whether they have firm convictions on the way to live an upright life.

Anyone can marry and have children, but to be a good parent is not easy; it requires great effort, both physical and spiritual. To be the best of all possible teachers to their children, parents must always seek to control and improve themselves. In other words, they must be prepared to learn and grow with their children.

When a couple's first child is born, they are of course glad to be parents, but they will not yet have that special attachment to their child that develops only with time. That attachment and love will deepen over the years as they devote themselves to the challenging process of rearing their child. In a way, parents and children are born at the same time. Raising children inevitably raises parents: only through the process of raising a child does one truly become a parent.

The cooperation of husband and wife is essential in raising children. Today, when many fathers are white-collar workers who spend most of their waking hours in an office and commuting, the time they can spend with their families is severely limited. But it remains very important that husband and wife discuss their children's upbringing. For example, they should discuss the way to teach the children proper study habits, clearly decide what role each parent will play in teaching the children, and have a good understanding of each child's character, potential, and abilities. Further, the parents should make sure that they themselves have a good attitude toward learning. If they do, the children will naturally imitate them and learn to study.

I have heard that in South Korea sugar is rarely used in cooking. Instead, Korean cooks use honey as sweetening. This practice may help explain why Korean children have fewer cavities than Japanese children. Children love sweets and apparently need a certain amount of sugar in their diet, but too much sugar harms their teeth and, it is said, weakens their bones. Substituting honey for sugar to reduce their children's sugar intake for the sake of good health is an example of the kind of concern for their offspring parents should demonstrate in every aspect of life.

Shakyamuni, the historical Buddha, taught that husband and wife must love and respect each other. Of course, some couples become upset from time to time and quarrel. They are apt to think that their children will not understand their quarreling and that therefore it will not harm them. But even if the children do not understand, they see and hear the quarreling and are very sensitive to the hostile atmosphere, which shocks them deeply, making them anxious, confused, and sometimes ill. Especially in front of their children, it is important that parents heed Shakyamuni's exhortation to love and respect each other, preserving the mutual respect that is the basis of love and harmony.

Social factors outside the home figure greatly in such problems as juvenile delinquency, violence in the schools, and juvenile suicides, but children's relationship with their parents is seen as the most important factor. In Japan children have traditionally been regarded as gifts of the gods and buddhas. Each child has his or her own individuality and human worth. Parents' actions must be based on a sound understanding of human nature, arising out of a reverence for all life, and they must do all they can to fulfill their roles of firm father and loving mother.

❧　　　❧　　　❧

We should strive to create the kind of home environment that enfolds family members in warmth and spiritual comfort. Constant tension in the home causes mental stress and weakens young people's will to grow and improve. Warmth and spiritual comfort do not, however, mean spoiling children or allowing them to do whatever they please. Sometimes it is essential to scold them severely and to point out the correct path.

The ability to understand children is essential in parents. They must constantly strive for the view that is not one-sided but all-embracing, that is farsighted and not blinded by immediate phenomena, and that grasps fundamentals rather than concentrates on superficial details. For instance, a parent who is obsessed with a child's disobedience may be blinded to the child's good traits. In such a case, the parent can become too emotional and criticize in ways so shocking and wounding that the child becomes despondent and then, in reaction, all the more stubborn and defiant.

Parents who are aware of their children's other traits will realize that disobedience is related to a growing sense of independence and will not lose sight of the children's good qualities, such as concern for brothers and sisters. These parents will be able to praise disobedient children for firmness of character. Such praise will give the children the satisfaction of having their good points recognized and will stimulate them to correct their failings.

No one is universally condemned. Similarly, since no one is perfect, no one is universally praised. It is only human to have both good and bad points. A home in which children hear nothing but reprimands for their shortcomings lacks spiritual comfort and therefore is unpleasant.

Consequently, parents and teachers must be able to distinguish between the faults that require immediate correction and those that should be overlooked until children can correct themselves. It is also important to have the wisdom to remain impartial and to deal with children in ways that recognize and develop their good points.

The home must be more than a place in which to relax and recover from fatigue. It must be a place in which we pay reverence to the gods and the Buddha, who are our spiritual mainstays, and strive for self-improvement by following their teachings. Such a home life will foster in the family members true spiritual well-being, a sense of fulfillment, and a reason for living. Creating a domestic environment filled with the spiritual comfort that allows young people to grow up wholesomely is the primary duty of adults, whose experience of life is greater.

BALANCING WORK
AND REST

In one of his works, Dogen (1200–1253), the founder of the Soto Zen sect in Japan, advocates the practice of sometimes thinking of nothing at all for a while. His intent is to help Zen trainees attain the tranquil state of meditation called *samadhi*, or concentration, in which the mind is free of all thought. But tranquillity and psychological refreshment are important in everyone's daily life.

If the stress associated with most of our activities is allowed to build up, it can express itself as anxiety or even illness, can spoil our relations with others, and can lead to errors in our work. It is vital to eliminate stress and thus deal with anxiety and restore vitality. To this end, time spent thinking of nothing is helpful, just as sleep is for recovery from fatigue.

Although experienced meditators can empty their minds of all thought merely by sitting still, an expert on zazen (seated meditation) once pointed out to me that for beginners inactivity of this sort breeds all kinds of random thoughts and leads to insecurity. Instead of trying to think of nothing while sitting perfectly still, it is easier to empty the mind by fully absorbing oneself in some interesting activity. This was explained to me by someone who becomes thoroughly absorbed in kendo, or Japanese fencing, practice.

When we are absorbed in what we are doing, our minds enter a state of concentration in which we are lost in thought. This state is a kind of *samadhi*. People can attain this state by engaging in a particular activity, either a strenuous one like a sport or a physically passive one like reading. Engaging in an activity that fully absorbs us brings about the change of pace we need in daily life and is therefore sound mental hygiene. Although it is good to be absorbed in our work, engrossing activities unrelated to work are likely to be more enriching. The amount of time spent in total absorption each day can greatly alter the way we live.

Periods of rest are essential to enable us to recover from fatigue and restore the energy we need for clear thinking. Rest is necessary in our religious activities, as well. Ceaseless diligence in religious practice is praiseworthy, but our practice can become mechanical. When religious practice becomes mechanical, it loses much of its power to move us or to inspire gratitude, and that can lead to discontent.

Many people claim to be too busy to take a vacation from work, but lack of relaxation causes

fatigue and robs us of vitality and the ability to
think clearly. Though it is best to allow ourselves
extended periods of rest for mental and physical
refreshment, if this proves impossible it is good to
set aside some time each day free from the demands
of our work. We should determine for ourselves
how to spend that time (perhaps talking with
friends or pursuing a hobby) to recover from fatigue at the end of the day and to regain energy for
the day to come.

People whose daily lives include some kind of
activity or hobby in which they can become fully
absorbed are very fortunate. Not all people are so
fortunate, however. For many, there can be no res-
pite from stress or difficulty. To maintain mental
and physical health, these people should rest or relax when they feel tired. Striking a balance between
activity and relaxation is most important.

Nothing equals the refreshed feeling we get from invigorating activities like sports. When we exercise
strenuously, the body's energy seems to be used as
efficiently as fuel is in perfect combustion. But
many people lack opportunities for such activities,
eat too much, or suffer from frustrations that lead
to an accumulation of stress. All these things result
in what we might term imperfect combustion of the
body's fuel, injure our health, and keep us from feeling mentally and physically alert.

We are often told that our bodies are adversely

affected by overreliance on modern conveniences, by synthetic fibers in our clothing, by additives in our foods, and even by the concrete apartment buildings in which more and more of us live. Instead of unthinkingly accepting the changes in our environment, we must protect our health in ways that take these factors into account. The traditional Japanese way of living in harmony with nature has much to teach us about healthful food, clothing, and housing. For instance, many traditional Japanese foods (such as the pickled plums that many Japanese eat almost daily) combine nourishment and medicinal properties.

Though good health is a major factor in happiness, it is not the only one. A person with a chronic or incurable illness or a severe handicap need not feel doomed to unhappiness. A great many members of society live each day fully and strive steadily to improve themselves as human beings despite illness or handicaps. I am always moved deeply by their stories and their efforts, which are precious examples of the essence of faith.

All these people have one thing in common: they refuse to be obsessed by illness or handicaps. They accept actuality for what it is and move forward from there. They are able to live each day in a positive, meaningful way because they have—in Buddhist terms—found liberation from actuality.

Conversely, healthy people can become so obsessed with something that they find it impossible to remain cheerful for long. This in turn harms their physical condition. Buddhism teaches that mind and body are intimately and indivisibly related. In the light of this teaching, it is obvious that we benefit from every attempt we make to be cheerful all the time.

Our attitudes have an immense influence on our physical health. People who grumble and are dissatisfied with their work are more likely to fall ill than others who go about the same tasks in a spirit of cheerful gratitude. From a religious viewpoint, falling ill always has meaning. The sick person who can examine the way of living and thinking that contributed to the illness is already on the road to recovery.

To maintain mental and physical health, it is an excellent idea to take a vacation from work, go out into fields or woods, and work up a good sweat. But since not everyone can do this, I offer two practical suggestions on ways of refreshing both mind and body.

First, walk three to five kilometers each day. When we walk, our bodies absorb several times the oxygen they would if we sat still indoors for the same length of time. Walking stimulates the brain and is good for the digestion. Philosophers and scientists have long commended walking.

Too many people rely more than they need to on private automobiles or public transportation. For instance, people who regularly travel by local buses can get more exercise if they walk a little farther and board their bus one stop beyond their regular stop or leave the bus one stop before their destination. Each time they take a bus, they should walk farther, until they find themselves walking three to five kilometers every day. Since physical and mental health are so closely related, weakness in the legs and thighs caused by inactivity and insufficient exercise can dull the mind.

Second, read your faith's scriptures aloud daily, breathing deeply and projecting your voice from your diaphragm. Daily oral scriptural reading should be combined with daily silent reading of favorite inspirational works.

By such means as these, we should all strive to improve our health so as to set a good physical and mental example for everyone we meet.

❦   ❦   ❦

Since good mental and physical health is not only a major factor in our happiness but also the foundation of all our activities, we should all have mental and physical examinations from time to time. Masahiro Yasuoka (1898–1983), who drafted the Showa emperor's radio-broadcast announcement of surrender that ended World War II and was a scholar of Wang Yangming (a Chinese school of learning), wrote that thorough psychological examinations are as significant to health as thorough physical examinations. In lieu of regular consultations with specialists, Yasuoka suggested that we ask ourselves the following questions every day:

1. Am I eating the right amounts of the right kinds of foods?

2. Am I getting enough sound sleep nightly?

3. Am I getting enough exercise?

4. Do I have any bad habits that affect my mental and physical well-being?

5. Am I easily upset by the problems of daily life or can I work as usual, whatever happens?

6. How much confidence do I have in my work?

7. Do I have a rewarding inner life?

8. Do I have truly good friends?

9. Do I keep certain good books by me all the time?

10. Do I have beliefs, precepts, and a faith of my own?

Fretting over everything that happens during a busy day often causes sleeplessness. To eliminate this source of sleeplessness, first reflect on the things that worry you, separating the important problems from the unimportant ones. Then decide how to deal with the important problems, and simply forget the others.

LIVING WITH NATURE

Uncontrolled economic development, which wreaks havoc on the natural environment, is a serious global problem threatening human survival. A cause of special concern everywhere is the rapid destruction of tropical rain forests through slash-and-burn agriculture and logging for export. It is said that the destruction is progressing so fast that an area of rain forest roughly one-sixth the size of Japan is lost each year. The consequences of this loss include the extinction of animal and plant species, floods, pollution of streams and rivers, and damage to the fishing industry.

Japan is the world's largest importer and consumer of timber from tropical rain forests. The bulk of the wood for disposable chopsticks, widely used in Japan, and for pulp to make tissue paper comes from the forests of Southeast Asia. This means that the Japanese cannot afford to look on the seemingly distant crisis of the world's rain forests as someone else's business. To fully restore the earth's rich green cover, we must do all we can to save the environment, the foundation of all life.

Of course, we need to fell a certain amount of timber, but the amount must be kept to a minimum. We can try to save the environment by protecting it, or ruin it by allowing greed to continue destroying forests unchecked.

In general, Eastern philosophy has tended to regard the universe as one in essence and to regard all things—including the natural environment and human beings—as essentially united and interdependent. In contrast to this approach, the West separates nature and humankind, and Western civilization has been influenced by the idea that humankind rules nature. Recently, however, many learned people in the West have come to see that the traditional Western view has reached an impasse, and they now strongly urge others to learn from Eastern wisdom in order to save humankind from ruin.

Although Western influence has predominated in Japan since the country was opened in the mid-nineteenth century, the Japanese have since ancient times traditionally revered nature, as is reflected in the Shinto religion, which, together with Buddhism and Confucianism, is part of the foundation of Japanese culture. Now that Japan is being blamed by many people in Southeast Asia for abetting the destruction of the rain forests, all Japanese ought to cultivate respect for nature by returning to their traditional Eastern, truly Japanese, way of thinking.

Effort even in small things can be important. For instance, for the past few years when I have eaten lunch in my office, I have avoided using disposable wooden chopsticks and instead have used a pair of bamboo chopsticks given to me by the leader of another religious organization. These are washed after each meal and can be used over and over. And they are convenient to carry. I realize that refraining from using disposable chopsticks is not enough to solve the problem, but I believe that concern in even small matters can grow into something big enough to save the natural environment.

Humankind can learn much from the workings of the great world of nature. Not even the fiercest animals kill indiscriminately. Yet humans, despite their intellectual powers, do precisely that in warfare and in environmental pollution, which now threatens the planet with destruction. To prevent the worst, we must learn from nature and cease upsetting the natural harmony. Furthermore, we must learn restraint from the great wisdom of the East.

Earth is said to have come into existence about 4.7 billion years ago. Life emerged, and after many ages the human race appeared. Historical records have existed for only some five thousand years. Now that we understand something of how our planet came into being, we at last begin to see how wonderful and blessed it is. People today must realize that their greatest mission is to protect their precious planet and its green cover, which took such an inconceivable length of time to evolve.

Recently many of the world's nations have been trying to limit the amounts of chlorofluorocarbons released into the atmosphere. Used as coolants in refrigerators and air conditioners and as propellants in aerosol spray cans, chlorofluorocarbons are destroying the stratospheric ozone layer, which absorbs ultraviolet rays from the sun. When the ozone layer weakens, more ultraviolet rays reach the earth, harming human beings, warming the atmosphere, and causing environmental changes that will be fatal to much plant and animal life.

Chlorofluorocarbons are but one example of the many ordinary domestic substances that become pollutants when used in large quantities. All such pollution offers clear evidence that the conveniences made possible by technology have side effects that wreak great damage on the environment, threatening all life. Each of us must reexamine our willingness to use these conveniences unthinkingly, despite the harm they cause. We must try to act effectively to protect the environment.

The Amish, a conservative Christian group in the United States, continue to maintain a seventeenth-century lifestyle. Supporting themselves by farming, they shun electricity, travel in horse-drawn buggies, and use horses to cultivate their fields. They adopt this simple way of life out of religious conviction. For those of us of other faiths, their way of living provides food for deep thought. First, the Amish represent humility guided by religion. Second, they show us the strength of conviction needed to preserve a style of life based on what is truly important to humankind.

Many European and North American families spend holidays in cottages in remote areas without modern conveniences. In such places, where even electric light is unavailable, these families not only rediscover themselves but also come to see the wastefulness of their ordinary lifestyle.

Determining whether modern conveniences are ultimately useful to humankind will take time. Nonetheless, it seems very likely that leaping to accept every new convenience and grasping at everything that saves labor will sooner or later invite serious trouble, and this is most disturbing.

Pollution starts with greedy individual behavior that, if persisted in, has a baleful influence on society at large. Ending pollution demands that individuals reexamine their lives. Unless they do so, we can hope for no solution at all.

Some scholars claim that the abundance of conveniences today makes people too inactive, so that their oxygen intake is less than it should be, which often depresses bodily functions and causes illness. This theory clearly points out the danger of relying too much on labor-saving devices.

There are many simple remedies. For instance, people who travel by city buses can exercise more by getting off a few stops short of their destination and walking the rest of the way. Although this takes time and is less convenient, it is decidedly better for the health.

Shunning modern conveniences like electricity

and automobiles may seem a negative approach but may actually be a very positive one in terms of health and environmental protection. People and their environment are one. From time to time it is a good idea to put up with some inconvenience in order to think about what is best for both.

Many of today's young Japanese reportedly suffer from such physical problems as stiff shoulders and nausea, although physicians find nothing wrong with them. Investigation from a different angle, however, has shown that most of these young people tend to disturb their biorhythm by staying up very late at night. In general, modern humans are becoming nocturnal in their habits, and that tendency is spreading from adults to an increasing number of children.

Earth, the home of so many different life forms, has always been subject to the rhythm of day and night. Like other animals living with this rhythm for millions of years, humans have developed an inner biological clock and are fundamentally diurnal in behavior.

Consequently, after sunset it is important to allow one's body to rest and recharge itself. And in the early morning it is good to provide the lungs with plenty of fresh, clean air. With this in mind, we can see that morning Buddhist devotions—sutra chanting or recitation, for example—benefit the body as well as the mind.

Since our biorhythm is that of a diurnal animal, it is only to be expected that staying up late at night will adversely affect our bodies. Some students preparing for examinations claim to study better at night, when it is quiet. But studying during the day when the body is more alert seems to produce better examination scores.

On a recent trip to Europe I happened to see a University of the Saarland research report on the extinction of a certain small insect. The report said that this seemingly irrelevant development actually relates to the continued survival of the human race. The disappearance of the small insect will reduce the numbers of larger insects that feed on it and of animals that feed on the larger insects. Eventually this development could seriously affect the supply of food available to humans.

Although we often think that we live independent of other forces, it is the great workings of nature that sustain us. For this very reason, we should respect nature and live in harmony with it so as to make the most of the life bestowed on us.

Recently more and more executives have been complaining of health problems. One reason for their problems is no doubt their tight schedules, which keep them busy day and night and place great demands on them physically and mentally. But even in the course of busy lives, we must pause and think whenever we feel that our rapid pace is upsetting our biorhythm.

Leading a healthy life is in keeping with Buddhist teachings on nature and humankind. A healthy life includes going to bed early, rising early, and closing the day with the whole family taking part in evening devotions in a spirit of gratitude. By doing these things regularly and at the natural time, Buddhists can lay the foundation of a wholesome life of faith.